D1118739

CROSS THE TRACKS

CROSS THE TRACKS

A Memoir

BOOSIE BADAZZ

Gallery Books
New York   London   Toronto   Sydney   New Delhi

Gallery Books
An Imprint of Simon & Schuster, Inc.
1230 Avenue of the Americas
New York, NY 10020

First Gallery Books hardcover edition June 2022

GALLERY BOOKS and colophon are registered trademarks of Simon & Schuster, Inc.

For information about special discounts for bulk purchases, please contact Simon & Schuster Special Sales at 1-866-506-1949 or business@simonandschuster.com.

The Simon & Schuster Speakers Bureau can bring authors to your live event. For more information or to book an event, contact the Simon & Schuster Speakers Bureau at 1-866-248-3049 or visit our website at www.simonspeakers.com.

Interior design by Matthew Ryan

Manufactured in China

10 9 8 7 6 5 4 3 2 1

Library of Congress Cataloging-in-Publication Data is available.

ISBN 978-1-9821-3136-4
ISBN 978-1-9821-3138-8 (ebook)

33614083010933

This book is dedicated to the ones I love and the ones I have loved and lost. There are a lot of people I have lost in these stories. Special shout-out to the babies in ghettos across the world.

To all the prisoners in jails everywhere: You are somebody. Don't give up because you're doing time. I've been there and made the change.

To my children, who will always be first in my life—Iviona Hatch, Tylayja Hatch, Torrence Hatch, Toriana Hatch, Ivy Ray Hatch, Lyric Hatch, Michael Hatch, Laila Jean Hatch—you mean the world to me.

"The Lord is my shepherd, I shall not want. He makes me to lie down in green pastures; He leads me beside the still waters. He restores my soul; He leads me in the paths of righteousness for His name's sake. Yea, though I walk through the valley of the shadow of death, I will fear no evil; for You are with me; Your rod and Your staff, they comfort me. You prepare a table before me in the presence of my enemies; You anoint my head with oil; my cup runs over. Surely goodness and mercy shall follow me all the days of my life; and I will dwell in the house of the Lord forever."
—PSALM 23, NKJV

"I can accept failure; everyone fails at something. But I can't accept not trying."
−*MICHAEL JORDAN*

CONTENTS

FOREWORD
BY CHARLES BURGESS

It is a miracle that Boosie is alive and with us today. In his mid-thirties, he has survived being shot at multiple times, teenage fatherhood, a prison term on death row, diabetes, and cancer. He has pulled through it all, relying on his faith in God.

It is a miracle for sure that the poor people Dr. King told us not to forget are the same poor people—like Boosie—who created hip-hop, the dominant popular culture on the planet since the late 1970s.

Boosie's music is not for everyone. He knew some would not like how raw and real he is—how he speaks about himself, about Black people, racism, women, violence, drugs, material things, and life and death. But if you take the time to read this book and truly hear Boosie's words, you will gain a greater understanding of and compassion for what it is to be Black and male in these United States. The vast majority of us grew up with little to nothing and had to survive with whatever was in front of us. In hearing his words, you will get, without question, the story of Boosie's America.

CROSS THE TRACKS

PROLOGUE

Me and my mom at Angola Prison in Louisiana.

Welcome to death row, 2010. *Clang!*

The sound of iron bars closing me in.

News reporters and the local Baton Rouge newspaper, the *Advocate*, were getting ratings and sales like they'd never seen before. The system had me. They wanted me to spend the rest of my life in jail. They alleged that I'd hired a hit man to commit murder. The same night they accused me of this crime, I was in my studio putting together some tracks to be released. "Body Bag" and "187" were being cut. Soon the lyrics to my songs would be on trial, as well as my body and soul.

No witnesses, a forced confession, and no DNA or physical evidence that would warrant a conviction, but there I sat at a table with my defense attorney pleading not guilty. Then they used against me the thing I loved most—my own music.

Yo Marlo / He got a Monte Carlo / That bitch Trey / I want that bitch dead / Here go the key . . .

I had spit that lyric metaphorically, as storytelling. It did not mean I paid someone money to do a crime. Marlo was a friend of mine. During an interrogation, he was told by police that I had even issued a hit on his life for twenty-five grand. Several corrupt law officials were set on making a case for murder. They interrogated this young man for hours, fabricating lies, then only recording what they wanted the courts to hear. In an even deeper speculation, they interpreted a tattoo on his arm to mean he was my hit man for hire, waiting on me to issue orders for him to carry out.

I was being charged with the murder of Terry Boyd. He was the uncle of my child that I'd fathered with his sister. The district attorney's case suddenly tanked when Marlo finally got on the stand and told under oath how the police had obtained his confession. Right after that, the police took the stand and denied what Marlo had said.

I knew all this was in retaliation for a track I'd released called "Fuck the Police." In it I mentioned almost every branch of law enforcement I could possibly think of—including the FBI and the district attorney. I had made them look bad, so they wanted revenge. That would have been their justice, to see me facing lethal injection.

Got old it got worser, my hustle got deadly / Runnin' and duckin' from dat dirty bitch Don Kelly . . .

That was a lyric in the first verse of "Fuck the Police." Don Kelly went on to become Captain Donald Kelly, giving the city thirty-two years of service. My verses told the tale of how they would pull me over and try to extort me for money. I went on to let them know how I felt with the chorus line:

Cities, FUCK 'EM!

Narcotics, FUCK 'EM!

FEDS, FUCK 'EM!

DAs, FUCK 'EM!

We don't need you bitches on our street say with me

FUCK DA POLICE! (fuck 'em!) FUCK DA POLICE! (fuck 'em!)

Witout dat badge you a bitch and a half niggah

I believe this song and the two songs I created the night Terry Boyd was gunned down were the seeds of a hate relationship between me and the Baton Rouge Police Department. Not because they had evidence linking me to a murder, not because they had their bogus statement, but because I had exercised my freedom of speech. Because a Black man had spoken truth to power in the American Deep South.

Chapter 1

BADAZZ BOOSIE, SOUTH BATON ROUGE– THE BEGINNING

Cross the Tracks thuggin'.

Cross the Tracks is what we call my hood. Being raised there gave me the morals I live by, my values on family and life, and most of all, my codes for hustling. As far back as eight years old, I was hustling. It's just what people from my neighborhood did.

My partners and I started knocking off the Circle K gas stations. We would stop there daily before hitting the schoolhouse. We would clean their candy aisles out, planning to sell what we stole. More than books, product lined our backpacks: Snickers bars, Reese's Cups, and all the flavors of Now and Laters. It became an easy thirty- to forty-dollar-a-day hustle for us. As an eight-year-old have-not, that was a lot of paper to be in your pocket. We were getting it.

After school, we would hurry to the crib to jump on our bikes. Riding our bikes all over town was our shit. I considered myself fortunate to even have a bike, especially since my father, Raymond Hatch, was a user. He played with the monkey, but I guess the monkey wasn't on his back like for most people who used. Raymond always made sure home was straight, to the best of his abilities. Me and my dudes all had reflector fetishes. It was a big thing back in those days to be riding your pedal cruiser with the sun beaming the brightest off your front wheel. Of course whoever got the most reflectors was deemed the man by the neighborhood girls. I stole so many damn reflectors . . . you get the point.

We'd ride until our stomachs growled with hunger, and there was only one place in town we would stop—Mrs. Mula's place. If you had six dollars, you didn't need McDonald's or Burger King. Mrs. Mula was so good at cooking that she should have had her own golden arches and her own slogan—*Over a billion ghetto plates served.* Her fried turkey wings and deep-fried pig tails could have put any casual dining chain out of business.

Her dilapidated home was like a real restaurant, and she made sure she had something for everyone's taste and budget. Flavored Dixie Cups for the shawties, an assortment of different candy; she even had pickles for the girls who liked to put peppermints down inside them and suck the juice. Hell, Mrs. Mula even sold pig lips, if that was what you liked. She was one hell of a cook and definitely a boss hustler.

So much came with the good, and so much more came with the bad. Crime, guns, and homicides plagued my environment like they were a natural part of life. Guns were easy to come by—entirely too easy. When I was just nine years old, my cousin shot my other cousin with a handgun. I had always thought all that blood you see in the movies was just some fugazi red coloring to make the scene more intense, to sell more tickets. How could a person bleed out so much and survive? But that day, I saw that shit was for real. My cousin didn't die, which was a good thing, but he sure spent four months in the hospital. That was the first really violent thing I saw in my early years.

Every kid had someone they looked up to. With drug dealer role models like Calvin Ricks and Kenny Wayne, there was always something to see. These big ballers were the men who had it going on, and they controlled the streets. They were like the Black Pablo Escobar and El Chapo.

At eleven, what most would consider to still be a tender age, I witnessed my first murder.

My friends and I were parked across the tracks like we normally would be after doing our bullshit—things like riding our bikes up to Louisiana State University or hanging out at the game room. Sometimes we'd just cruise to the levee to throw rocks at cars passing by; that was when we were on some really dumb shit. There were times when we felt like young playas and would hit the Roosevelt Projects to either chase a young cutie-pie to see how far we could get, or just mess around and play some basketball.

On this particular day, we were just chilling on our bikes. We watched the local kingpins making their money. The air smelled like rain even though the sun was shining bright. In the Dirty South, you never know what Mother Nature is up to. Like any other woman, she always has her own agenda. Rain one day, sunny the next, or sending hurricanes like Katrina through to show who is the real boss. Baton Rouge was known to go from sunshine to a flood in a heartbeat.

While chilling on the railings, we peeped a dude rolling up slow and smooth on his bike. He was calm and cool. The dude he was approaching was also chilling and none the wiser, until the rider called his name like he was his friend. The target turned around and all you heard was *pop-pop-pop-pop*. The orange blaze blossomed out the barrel of the pistol as the first four shots entered the target's chest, then sent the helpless man tumbling over. Just to be certain, the shooter let loose two more rounds up close. The deal was sealed and the victim was a dead man.

What's crazy is it wasn't out of the ordinary for things like that to happen. In my hood that was normal, everyday life. Cross the Tracks had seen endless mayhem and murder. It felt like the thing to do when my friends and I went over to the corpse and emptied the dead man's pockets.

Chapter 2

GROWING UP IN THE BLOODY RED STICKS

Hustling was a way of life for real. There was always gambling and drug selling, which were a given, but one legitimate hustle in my hood was food. I've already spoken on Mrs. Mula, who had the everyday food business on lock in the community, but people also did what we called *suppers.*

These were gatherings where someone would throw down on the grill or prepare dishes to be sold at a backyard get-together. Music would be blaring out of speakers like a concert was going on, and you could see some of the finest girls from the neighborhood there. Most of the time, they would come from all over because they knew the men with the deep pockets and fly whips would be hanging around. These chicks would be dressed to impress, wearing their tight-fitting booty shorts, designer minidresses, and the latest fresh Nikes. The chicks spared no expense, from their wardrobes to their hairdos.

Suppers were a way for people to do a little better than just make ends meet. There would be gambling going down at these suppers—rolling dice, different card games, and dominoes. Everything had a wager on it. The person throwing the supper was considered the house, like at a casino, and they took a rake too. In the hood we called it the cut money.

A typical supper consisted of a simple menu: fried catfish, potato salad, and bread. Some people whipped out the grills, getting fancy with burgers and slow-cooked ribs. It was an amazing thing, though, to see people in the hood coming and supporting each other. Some came just to gamble and some just to check out the eye candy, but it didn't matter who you were. When there was a supper, you were invited. It was all about the Benjamins, and save the drama for another day. Suppers were a tradition going back to at least the early sixties. Food and gambling were the bedrock foundation of Cross the Tracks.

■ ■ ■

It seemed to me that if you grew up in South Baton Rouge, either one or both of your parents were substance abusers. Drugs were second nature in the hood and a primary coping mechanism. That monkey was on the back of almost every adult in the community at one time or another. Shooting cocaine was as commonplace as sipping water. It seemed normal, but if you indulged in that lifestyle, you had to maintain it—and that meant selling dope.

It seemed like all the women were attracted to the men who pushed coke. The cream of the crop weren't fucking around with a broke man when they could have a dope man, one who was sending them to the mall to shop or to the beauty salon to get themselves together—hair, nails, whatever they wanted. If you were into the high-class—or should we say "so-called high-class," ghetto-fabulous-type chicks—you needed money in my city. It was Cross the Tracks business as usual.

Sundays had a different atmosphere in the hood. The park would be full of people playing softball or basketball, having a good time. No doubt, food would be everywhere and available—I'm surprised there weren't more obese people, as much as everyone ate. This was a day the young could hustle as well. We would scout the cars, basically looking for the drug dealers who had even the smallest specks of dirt on their rides. These cats took pride in their whips, especially when they were on the prowl. It was easy for us to hustle up on some soap and water and wash their cars, Johnny-on-the-spot.

It wasn't always all good in the hood, though. We had sad times, like when somebody lost their life and had to be buried. Funerals in my hood were like those in a lot of other Southern towns. Everyone would come out to pay their respects to the deceased. Family, no matter what, was strong. We respected that by showing up. There were a lot of murders and deaths. You had to be hard to the core, because surely there wasn't an in-between for you. If you were hard, you earned your respect. If you were soft, let's just say problems were going to find you. People knew who—and who not—to fool with.

I learned a lot from my father, Raymond, even though he used drugs. Before he'd go off on any binge, he made sure that family was handled. He took care of home first and partied second. I had to respect him for that. My mother, Connie, also held down a job, as a schoolteacher. I guess you can say, despite the problems we had, I still came from a loving set of parents. We didn't have much as far as material things, but what we did have, we learned to be grateful for. Because there was a multitude of young ones who didn't have a pot to piss in or a window to toss it out of.

Raymond had bought my bike, which was my pride and joy. Every time I rode, I felt like I had a Mercedes-Benz. All the reflectors we stole for our bikes were like when the ballers had fancy cars to attract the women. The more reflectors you had beaming from your spokes, the more side-glances from the girls.

The LSU campus was always the perfect spot to come up on a female or a hustle. The college kids would park and chain their bikes up to one of those metal racks. We would wait until the coast was clear, then we would snatch all the reflectors off their spokes in seconds. When we rode at night, the streetlights would shine down, making it look like Christmas trees were rolling down the block. We would ride all over the city, including out to a place called Catfish

Town. Those times made it seem not so bad to be an adolescent from Cross the Tracks.

Life was crazy coming up. When you're trying to come up and win, everybody acts like that is what they want for you. But once you climb that ladder, put in that work, and become that man, the same people turn on you. They be the same ones hating that you made it—dudes ten years your senior on about some old beef that didn't make sense. Most of the time, it would be some made-up shit, just to get something started. One thing I was true to was being a soldier, and I didn't care what it was about. I wasn't a punk and I was ready to handle the beef situations, especially when I got a little older and was on that PCP and a few other choice drugs.

When I was hustling at like seventeen, I thought ten or twenty grand was a lot of money to make. A couple of times when that thirty grand rolled in, I was like, "Yeah, this that real paper!" But it wasn't until I turned nineteen and made my first hundred pack that I felt like I was holding some real cash. Things were always about locking down the deals to keep the checks coming. As I grew and started to learn things, I found there were more ways, more deals to be made, that would allow checks to come in.

Guns were something that had always been around. You could find guns at my house, my aunt's house, my cousin's place, or even up under my grandmother's porch. We felt the guns would protect us and our people in case we had trouble. Then, when I had my daughter, I wanted to be around to raise her, so I had to stay protected out there. I wanted to give my child everything, and that was a plan I knew I was sticking to. I was surviving day by day, never thinking about the future. Bullets were flying over my head like mosquitos, but I kept heat because I had to get to the next check for my daughter.

I was a hustler, so that's what I was on. The hustle made me feel how a lot of other Black men felt: because we had seen so many hurt or taken out with our own eyes, our deaths were probably right around the corner. "When it's my turn . . ." Those words echoed in our heads, and we started predicting when, how, and why we would meet our Maker. When the friends you're with every day start going by the wayside, that's when these thoughts really start to haunt you.

Chapter 3

MY MOMMA
AND MY DADDY

Waka Flaka and my mom in 2012.

As far back as I can remember, my momma, Connie, aka T-Lady, was an avid Bootsy Collins fan. Listening to his records, she couldn't conceal that beautiful smile of hers. Boy, if you could have seen the way music used to move her, especially B.C. This man was like a hero in her eyes. Through his music, he comforted her and gave her a sense of protection, which I found inspiring. That's exactly how the birth of the name Lil Boosie came about.

Most of the time when she and my father got into their little disputes, to drown him out she'd pull out her Bootsy Collins and allow it to soothe her mind. There were times I'd catch her swaying to the beat, gliding gently across the floor as if being led by an invisible partner. Throughout my years of growing up, I found myself following in those footsteps—trying to be her comforter, hero, and provider. It was only right, being that she truly deserved it.

Just as the life I chose created obstacles for me, I realized it had been hard on her as well. Like the countless times law enforcement would assault our front door with the heels of their boots, having no respect for her house while doing their drug raids. Not to mention how negatively my name flowed out of folks' mouths. What parent wants to hear their child's name being dragged through the mud, whether or not the rumors are true? It would have to feel as though they've failed as a parent.

Now, my mother, knowing her worth, would never consider herself to be a failure, even if I did stray. She always identified herself as a complete woman, with the belief of instilling love into her family. One thing I can say about that woman is she loves her children to life, and she cherishes the time, moments, and memories with her grandchildren. She's the purest of the bloodline and has always been my rock. Although we're two different spirits, we connect as one soul, so when she hurts, I hurt.

I think the saddest of our shared moments was when she lost her mother. Of course it ripped me apart to lose my granny—she meant the world to me—but it broke me even more to see the impact her death had on dear Momma. Never had I seen her show such pain before that day. From the top of her lungs, she released a scream that made me feel as if she was checking out on me. She did this until her lungs were too tired to continue and she had grown hoarse. Words cannot possibly describe the love I have for my momma, T-Lady.

My momma is a small woman in stature. She only stands about five-two, but she's my energy all day, every day. Ever since I can remember, she's been there consoling and protecting me, even though I'm supposed to be her hero. Every time I lay eyes on her, it reminds me that I'm blessed with the greatest mom ever. You know the rare type, the kind of mother who wouldn't dare place herself before her kids. She's always been there, a cigarette in one hand and the other hand on her hip. Since the first time I opened my eyes, my momma's been a smoker. She maintained it for many years—guess we all need a stress reliever.

Now, as for my daddy, yours truly is the spitting image of him. He had a midnight complexion, and he overshadowed me at five-nine. In his eyes, that alone meant I should look up to him. His build was comparable to mine, but his physique was a bit more toned and displayable for the women.

I love my parents, no question, but when it comes to my momma, she gets a standing ovation. She did the whole bid with me when I was in prison. Never once did she miss a scheduled visit. She even made sure my kids were in attendance every weekend, and that meant the world to me. Black women are blessed with a strength that men don't realize.

Women know they must be the backbone of the family, because they see firsthand how the men are lost in these streets. Mothers determine how their household is shaped. A man who spends more time outside the house will never be in alignment with how the inside of the home is run. His actions will always have the household sideways. It will never be one hundred percent in your house as long as you got a daddy who's in the streets, but a good momma will make sure it stays at least fifty percent right. I tip my hat to that kind of woman.

My momma worked two jobs to pay the bills and maintain our stability. She was a wife, a momma, and took care of the house. That meant going to games, parent-teacher conferences, field trips, and so forth. It was as if we breathed through her. Our lives were her life. You could see she was tired and drained, but she would always say, "As long as my kids don't have to worry about nothing, I'm good." I don't know how she was able to do all this, but she is the source of my strength.

It's so important for kids to be blessed with good parents. If a child doesn't have a good momma, that home will surely deteriorate, and it's hard for a single Black mother to maintain mentally, physically, and spiritually. But most of the time, she will—without any help at all. Struggles will come, especially if there are boys in the house. How can we expect women to raise boys into men? Yet and still, a single Black mother should know that she is that piece of the pie, even if she is underappreciated.

I witnessed my momma fight daily to maintain two jobs. I saw this woman repeatedly beaten, but she never lost the strength to care for us. It's so wrong for a woman to be degraded while providing for a child who cries for supper. My momma was never one to leave me in the care of others while she bounced from club to club. She was a stay-at-home mom. She never turned her back on us. She was always there, at all times.

Now, she *would* make her presence known during family gatherings. She'd show up, dance, and have the time of her life, but as far as going out to clubs? That was a no-no. Her personal life was always last on her list. She stayed home with us, waiting on Daddy to walk through those doors.

There were many nights Daddy, for his own reasons, chose not to come home. Two or three nights would go by and still he was a no-show. On those nights when she knew she'd be sleeping alone, her attitude would intensify. You could see the pain in her eyes as she paced the floors or did major cleaning just to keep busy. Me, personally, I chose not to speak to my momma during those times. But no matter how mad she was, every time Daddy showed back up, she'd let him right back in. For some reason, he always seemed to have a tiredness about him when he returned.

My father was truly a rolling stone. Wherever he decided to lay his hat definitely became his home. He couldn't sit still like Momma. Unlike her, he always had to be on the go, always into something. I must say though, he was a jack-of-all-trades. He did it all, from selling dope and crack to smoking primos and gambling—I mean, the whole nine yards. Baton Rouge is pretty small, so more than likely all our dads did dope together. I know for a fact that my friends Marcus's and John's fathers smoked with mine. So, nine times out of ten, your pops banged needles with our pops as well.

I don't know why women submit themselves to such abuse. I couldn't begin to tell you why my mother chose to put up with it for so long, but she did. I think it was for the sake of my brother and me. She refused to allow her kids to grow up fatherless, even if it meant crashing into a few brick walls. Eventually things became unrepairable. I was twelve or thirteen when she decided to make that call.

Before it got to that point, Momma had her some moments too. I can remember several occasions where Momma was like, "Fuck that shit! I'm tired. I can't do this anymore. I'm done." Then she'd leave. My brother and I would be tripping out, like, "What the hell is going on?" We would look to Daddy and be like, *Niggah, what you do this time?* Sometimes she would take us with her, and we would go stay at a motel until she regained her sanity. We'd go stay at the Motel 6. Momma never said why we had to go, and I never asked. The first night at the motel, I'd be quiet, but the second night . . . the second night was when we'd let the fun come out. That's because we knew we were going to be able to swim.

Other times she drove Daddy off, going in on him: "I can't stand that bitch, Ray! You make me sick, bitch. Are you crazy or something?" When she got hysterical like that, I'd get scared. My heart would just start beating uncontrollably. The fear mainly came from my daddy. When he got mad, he'd start beating on the door and throwing shit everywhere, just tearing up all the things my mother had worked so hard to get. He'd then leave and go stay at a hotel for a couple of days, but eventually, he'd come back.

I can remember this one time they got into a dispute and he actually burned my momma's Bible. Yes, my daddy went to the extreme on that one! *Like, who burns a Bible?* I think I was about eight or nine years old, something like that. I can remember it as clear as yesterday. Whenever they beefed, she would always run and get the Bible. I think she just did it because she knew it made him mad. She would always say to him, "I just can't be worried about you. I'm going to pray for you; that's what I'm going to do."

The Bible was sitting in the living room at the time. They'd just gotten into an argument and things were starting to get intense. He knew how she looked to the Word for strength, so he figured it would quiet her down and she would see how serious he was. He rushed into the living room, snatched up the Bible, and made his way out the front door to the porch. Before you knew it, *poof* . . . it was gone.

My momma was talking mad shit after that. "Look at this niggah. You think you did something? My hands are tied, my brotha. You gotta answer to God for that one. That's the Word of God, so it's like you just lit a match and shoved it in His mouth."

Things settled down for a few days after that, but the following week, they were back at it again. Somehow, my brother got involved this time. He had assumed Daddy had put his hands on Momma, and he became part of the situation; later, he found out Daddy hadn't done that after all. At the time though, it was just a big mess.

My momma just wanted me to be happy. Everything she did, she did to make sure I wasn't sad. It tore her apart to see me sad. She hated those moments when I wanted something and she couldn't afford to pay for it. That's when she would press herself the most; you understand what I'm saying? That's when I used to be asking for things all the time. But then it got to the point where I was tired of asking my momma for things. It was time for me to start helping my momma out. A man never really gave my momma anything, so I wanted to be the first man to place a thousand dollars in her hand.

That was something I'd always *wanted* to do, but when the time came for Daddy to look up at the world from his back, it was something I *had* to do. I hit the streets like a wrecking ball, knocking down everything that stood in the way of my success. I didn't want my momma to get too suspicious, so I'd only give her bits and pieces of cash here and there. I wanted to come clean so bad, because if she knew, that would give me a clear path to hustle and I could really make things happen. Instead I tried my best to hide it, but Momma wasn't stupid; she knew. She came to me one day and was like, "You think I'm stupid, boy, but I'm your momma; I raised you. You can't hide shit from me." Every time she said that, I would ask her what she meant. She would never respond. All she would do was walk past me and give me this crazy-ass look.

One day she got tired of the secrets and just flat out asked me, "Are you selling drugs?" I didn't want to lie to her because like I said, I had a better chance of succeeding with her knowing than not, so I said yes. Her reply couldn't have been clearer: "Get the fuck out of this house."

I went upstairs and began packing my blue suitcase. It was times like these when I missed the presence of my father. True, he could be a bit of an asshole, but he always meant well.

I remembered back to the time of his health crisis. At first, they didn't even want to let me into his hospital room, but my uncle said, "Let that niggah in! Hell, he needs to see his father. Who knows if he'll ever get this opportunity again?" With that said, my grandmother escorted me into his room. As I entered, it felt as though my legs were giving out on me. I was known for my cocky persona, so I didn't want to look weak in front of my family. I quickly pulled myself together. As we entered, all I could see was Daddy's eyes rolling to the back of his head. He was dying and there was nothing I—or anyone else—could do about it.

I gathered up enough strength to make my way to his bedside. The closer I got, the more the pain he seemed to be in. I loved my daddy and I didn't want to see him go, especially not like this. He had his ways, but he was a mighty warrior in my eyes.

I knew my time with my daddy was limited, but I had a few things he needed to know before he was on his back looking up at the world. I told him how much I loved him and how much his presence was respected and would be missed. He never knew the desire I carried for him to be proud of me. I felt the need to explain to him that I knew the value of being a man and that I was more than prepared to step up and take care of the family. I let him know I was going to make something out of myself and that one day, I'd be famous, someone the world would remember.

I knew he was listening and his facial expression confirmed that he believed every word. With that, I was satisfied. I kissed him on the forehead and took a few steps back to honor those last moments we'd shared together. I held it together because my people needed me to, but deep inside, I really wanted to fuck some shit up. I knew what my responsibilities would be once he'd passed, but dealing with the situation at hand was what I wasn't prepared for. To stand in front of one you love deeply, watching life slowly leave their vessel— now, that's an experience. It's true that Momma tended the garden, but Daddy had planted the seeds.

I can remember when I was about four or five years old and he'd make me walk around the house for hours with his shoes on. If I fell, he would make me get back up and keep going. When it was time to take them off, he'd ask me, "How was it?" I'd tell him it was hard and he'd say, "Tough shit! Deal with it. That's no comparison to the world you'll soon enter. It will push, pull, tug, knock you down, and trample all over you, testing your manhood. So, know that a man isn't a man just because he comes of age. Being a man comes with experience and sacrifices." See, shit like that was why I needed him here with me. There were a lot of things we never had the chance to discuss. The reason for that was fear. I didn't really know the right approach, because like I said, my father could be a muthafucka. If you caught him during one of those times he didn't want to be fucked with, that was your ass.

Chapter 4
MY FIRST LOVES

Me and my daughter Lyric celebrating her birthday
the day before I went to prison. She was ten months
old, so we had to throw her party early.

My first love had come about in middle school, her name was Mariea. We attended Kenilworth Middle School together. That was back when I was in the seventh grade, and that fly honey was a year ahead of me in the eighth grade. I was already a hot boy with the girls in school, but when I saw her, my jaw dropped. I guess you can say I was like that about females from an early age. If I saw one who caught my attention, I had to have her. I did whatever it took to get her. It was the same later in high school, with my ultimate flame, Walnita.

It was the middle of my eleventh grade year when I met Nita. There was a club where the teens went to get their groove on called the Zone, which was where I first met her. I was with my man Kevin, and as soon as I saw her, I tapped Kev and said, "I got to have her."

Kev knew I was serious. It was a lot of work to get her because she had this thing where she didn't want to be in competition with other girls. She would always say that all the other girls in the city liked me. She was right, but I still wanted her.

I would see Nita about three times a month, and every time I got the chance to see her, she would play hard to get. I kept up the pursuit, but that same year I got expelled. I ended up at an alternative school, Valley Park, where I met a chick named Brandy. I figured she and Nita were best friends, because every time I saw Nita at the Zone, I saw Brandy with her. That gave me the chance to get at Brandy about hooking me up with her girl. Every day in class, I would badger her about making the connection.

Nita was just that damn fine, her caramel-complexioned skin tone had me at attention every time I pictured her face. Nita was shapely—I mean, curves like a grown woman, or even better than most of the grown women I knew. Brandy must have gotten tired of me; she would tell me I was getting on her nerves, and I kept getting on them, until finally she dropped Nita's digits on me. When she gave me the number, it was a week after I had seen them at the club. Brandy must have gotten on her about me because when she did give me the number, she said, "Nita said call her."

After a few weeks of chopping it up on the phone, she came to see me and had Brandy with her, who visited my man Kev. We were hanging out on Garfield Street, doing what we do. She was looking good as fuck on her grown-woman shit. I mean her hair was fixed up real nice, nails looking like she'd just left the nail shop, and the pants she had on looked like the designer had made them just for her. They were tight, hugging each curve, demanding attention. All sorts of thoughts were floating through my head when I looked at her.

Things were taking a turn for the better . . . until that next week when we went to a place called the Plantation. After the club let out, this chick named Tracey and her twin sister jumped in my car, and Nita saw it. She was so pissed that when I called her, she hung up on me, leaving me staring at the phone like, *For real?* I hurried and dropped the twins at their destination and flew by Nita's house. I had to explain myself to her, or at least try to. It was late, maybe one in the morning, and as scared as I was, I still knocked on the door. My heart dropped when the door opened and there was her mother standing there. That was a little disrespectful, for a boy to be coming to your house at one in the morning for your teenage daughter. To my surprise, when I asked to speak to her daughter, after looking me up and down, she called Nita to the door.

Nita appeared in a see-through gown with some white slippers on her feet and her entire body smelling like roses. Her hair was still whipped and her two front golds shined. I went right into what I had come for, explaining that I didn't want Tracey. It was tough because she must have known that I'd once fucked around with Tracey. I told Nita straight up that I hadn't asked for the twins' company; they had just jumped in the car.

Her momma reappeared, and for a second it had me nervous all over again, wondering what she was going to say. She looked at both of us before saying to me, "Baby, you don't have to stand outside; you can come in." I walked inside, and Nita looked even better now that she wasn't behind a screen door.

In the living room, I saw pictures of Nita and what must have been her man or her ex. But I smiled because I knew I was her next. Besides, it wasn't a young niggah in Baton Rouge that had anything on me. I was the talk of the town and the flyest young dude around. We sat on the couch and spoke for about an hour. After I figured I was back in her good graces, I got up and went home. I didn't try to kiss her, catch a feel, or nothing. At that point I was just glad to be back in.

More visits followed. It became so frequent that I was at her crib every night. I remember this one particular visit like it was yesterday. It was late and it was pouring outside, raining cats and dogs, and I was about to get myself together to head home. Her mother looked at me, and she shocked the total shit out of me with what she said.

"Baby, you can spend the night. It's raining too bad to be out there in that mess."

It was the first time any of my girlfriends' mothers told me I could spend the night. I was so used to climbing through windows that it blew me away to have permission. Without hesitation I said, "Thanks, I'm staying here." I thought she was going to go grab some blankets and make up the couch, but she went on about her business and let me and Nita go about ours.

All those kisses I'd held back weren't being held back that night. That see-through gown wasn't much of a barrier, and Nita's bed was just the right size to keep us close. I couldn't wait to make love to her. I had been doing a lot of fucking, but I was ready to try to make love. I moved my hands slowly, taking my time, making her lose her breath. I could feel she was with it and just as excited as I was. We made love for the first time that night.

Five months later, Nita told me she was pregnant. I was excited that I was about to be a daddy. I knew I would be a good father, and that was all I could think about for the next couple of months. I had always had the notion that Nita and I were meant for each other. She and my mother had the same born day, March 16, and to me there was something special about that.

That first March 16 we got to spend together, we had some real fun. I had bought her a Tommy outfit and some matching perfume to go along with it. At the house, my momma saw it first. Since it was her born day too, she naturally thought it was a gift for her. When I said it was for my girl, all she could do was laugh. If there was anyone who knew me well, it was my momma.

It wasn't long after that that I started staying with Nita and her momma at their home, which turned out really cool. I used to sit in her room and smoke, and her mother was really chill about it. Louennia was her name, and she had become like a second mother to me—just without all the rules, so you know I was liking that. I loved the fact that Louennia was always cooking something, especially since I stayed high with the munchies. Nita had some skills burning too. I eventually moved out and got my own spot on Roosevelt Street, and Nita would come chill with me every day and cook something. My favorite dish was her rice and eggs. I used to be on her about it all the time, until she got sick of making it. It was my on-the-grind dish while we waited for our child to be born.

That day arrived on December 4, 2001. Iviona was born, and my God, she was such a beautiful baby girl. I was overwhelmed with joy to see my daughter happy and healthy. She and her mother quickly became my heart, my joys, my new reason to grind even harder. Nita and I had started building a life together—you know, that type of life you dream about when you think you have found your soul mate. There was nothing we wouldn't do together as a unit. We'd travel to other countries together, make business decisions together, and have everything our hearts desired together.

What amazed me about my child's mother was that she was tough. She had to be to have stuck with me through the thick and thin, the good times and bad times. I knew I was a lot for anyone to handle. She even went on to give me two more children, Ivy Ray and Michael Jordan. I took her through rough patches—like cheating on her, for instance—but she was ride-or-die for real. I say that because any other chick I'd dealt with ended what we had when I cheated. Nita would end it too, but then end up right back in my arms.

Her genuine concern for my career helped me know how much she cared. She was on my side, and when I wanted to quit the rap game at times, it was Nita who looked me in the eyes and said I couldn't. I will always have a deep-rooted love for the woman who I went through so much with—and who I took through so much.

At seventeen, I felt like a real man dealing with her. She already knew how to hold me down like a king, so everything else was like a bonus to the connection we had. I felt like I had a woman in Walnita—a real, grown woman who knew her shit. She had obviously taken her ways after her mother. She was the queen who I thought would be in the kingdom forever. Looking back, we all know, living the life I was living, that nothing was going to be forever. I ended up going to prison and that was the beginning of the end.

We hustled hard together, and I eventually moved her out her mother's house. We weren't forced to leave, but it was the right thing based on our lifestyles. We relocated to an air mattress in a one-bedroom project unit, in my hood Cross the Tracks. Nita was quite the cook, the best lover, and the best seducer I've ever been with. She'd make a meal, run my bathwater, and have everything laid out for me.

These standards of caretaking were hard for any woman to compare with. In a lot of ways, they reminded me of my grandmother's generation. Women were different back in Grandma's day, so to find one in this day and age who measured up said a lot about that female's character. Similarly, Nita had no problem speaking her mind. If I thought I was going to just run her over, I had another thing coming.

In 2010, we both ended up with a case and that was the breaking point for her. She held on as long as she could, but a woman has no place behind bars. As much as I expected her to hold her own, she couldn't. She ended up giving a confession that she was bringing drugs to the prison and doing some hustling herself, and they ended up locking us both up.

After twelve years of being together and ten years under the same roof, I truly loved her. She bore three of my seeds, Iviona, Ray Ray, and M.J. Even to this day, I miss her tenderness and thug passion, but she is married now and we've both moved on. I still love her, but I'm no longer in love, and I respect her situation. I will miss the way she treated me. Even if I never find that same mix of tenderness and thuggish style again, she set the bar on what I expect from a woman.

Walnita isn't the only woman who has given birth to my children. In total, there are five women who have kids by me. This was extremely hard. It wasn't hard being a father and taking care of my children—I made sure I had them all on holidays and summers—that wasn't the issue. It was the competition that started to brew between the women. When a man cuts off the dick supply to a baby-momma, all sorts of childish shit begins happening. They make it seem like there are issues with the kids just to get you off your square. I tried to minimize the smoke by keeping my little head in my pants when it came to these women. Sometimes it worked, sometimes it didn't.

I don't really communicate with them unless it's about the kids, but we keep it friendly and on a co-parenting level. I don't encourage any man to go out and have multiple baby-mommas just because he can. That is a headache I don't recommend. I was lucky to be able to handle the situation financially. I was once served papers by two of them, but we resolved that. I make sure I share the wealth with my seed and the mothers. I give them all the same amount of money each month. Nobody can use their amount to taunt the other ones, I make sure of that. I also make sure my kids want for nothing. I know firsthand how it is growing up wanting for things.

I thought before I went to jail that I had made my last child, but I had more. I wanted all my children to be winners in life, so I named them after some real winners: I named one of my sons Michael Jordan Hatch, and one of my daughters Lyric Beyoncé. Sometimes as a child, you need a drive and push beyond what a loving parent can give. I figured something as simple as a name could fuel that motivation. My son is going to be playing me in my movie and I'm proud of that. I was always a believer in my grandmother's words, and one cliché she used to kick around was "If you speak 'til they get it, it will happen." That is what propelled me to name my kids after people I deemed winners.

I've always wanted to tell my children's mothers that because of my kids, I'm a better man today. I know I can sometimes get on the internet and say a lot of things, but the truth is I don't regret any of those women or the times they spent in my life and that I spent in theirs. Experience is a motherfucker. At the same time, it can help you beat karma. I respect all we went through, and I feel wholeheartedly that if I hadn't gone through the things I did with them—and engaged in fatherhood—I would still be trapped in the prison system. For that reason alone, I'm grateful for the women who entered my life, for whatever reasons they chose.

I tell each of them, "Thanks for opening your legs," because that is how I talk, but they all know I mean the blessings that came from them doing so. They know how I am and how reckless I speak, but I really don't mean any harm by it. Bottom line is, God saw fit to put us in each other's path, and from that came the greatest gifts of all.

Chapter 5

BLOOD OF MY BROTHER

My brother, Taquari, preceded me by two years and ten months. As kids coming up, we were enlightened on family values and principles. "Family first!" were the words my mother assured us would protect us and keep us aligned. She repeatedly reminded us that never allowing the mud to separate the cement is what keeps the walk solid. Meaning, nothing should ever become a wedge between two brothers. They are of one mind, one body, and one spirit, which connects them. Her sentiments were understandable, but I have to agree to disagree because Taquari and I were like night and day. Competition was our operative word, and our whole childhood was like the Olympics. I mean, everything was a competition, from video games to sports to dancing. Believe me when I tell you we were total opposites with nothing in common.

Taquari was more intelligent than I was. I guess that's why he was placed in private schools while I was stuck in the public schools trying to find a way out. I always wondered what it would be like to attend his school. One time when he heard me say that, he quickly blurted out, "You wouldn't last a day at my school."

I jolted my head back a bit and was like, "Really? And what makes you think that?"

He shook his head slowly, staring in disbelief. "For one, your decision-making skills are pathetic. That alone would be reason enough for the students to distance themselves from you. I mean, have you looked at yourself? You'd walk up in that building and stand out like a sore thumb."

I told him that was exactly what I wanted, to be the center of attention. He looked at me like I was crazy before telling me he hadn't meant that in a good way and walking off.

I understood what he was saying. I followed the trends. I lived by the code of the streets, which meant I wouldn't be caught dead in his private school attire. No matter what we tried, we couldn't find anything that connected us. We couldn't even bond through music. While I was listening to 2Pac, Snoop Dogg, C-Loc, Concentration Camp, Scarface, and the Geto Boys, he was listening to Jay-Z, DMX, the Lox, Wu-Tang Clan, and Nas.

We can even go as far as talking about women. The girls he liked were gorgeous, elegant, and intelligent. Me, I was into those rough- necks, the types of girls who loved to scrap up and talk shit about anything. You know, the ones who were into dudes with my type of swag. In my eyes, Taquari always thought he was superior.

I can remember back, I think It was like 1998 or something. It was during the wintertime and we were outside having a snowball fight. Yeah, I can admit it, I was on some devious shit; I took a snowball and buried a stick inside it. Once I got him in range, I gave him one of those Pedro Martínez pitches and hit him right in the eye. Of course I got in trouble for it. That was the thing: he hardly got any spankings, but I found myself in the crosshairs continuously with my dad. Everyone always said I was the one who'd started it.

My brother knew how to get under my skin. He'd say things like "You'll probably be dead before you graduate, and that's if you'd graduate." Sometimes he'd even tell me I was a nobody and would never amount to anything. Those were the kind of low blows he threw. I must say, it truly let me know how he felt toward me.

I remember one time while we were in California I put faith in him and allowed him to cut my hair. He gave me one of those bowl cuts, which had everyone laughing at me, even him. He pushed me to the limit with that one, so I went and bleached all his clothes. Naturally, we ended up fighting, but I didn't care. Now when I look back at some of the things we did, I can smile about it, but not at that time. But it wasn't like that all the time. Sometimes we got along fine, especially when Daddy would come in drunk, trying to fight Momma. Taquari would hug me and tell me not to cry, everything will be all right, and I loved him for that.

I wanted to be like him so much. Either him or my cousin Trell. Now, Trell was a straight gangster. I remember one day I was testing my big brother's patience. I wouldn't stop bothering him and he ended up snapping out on me. He walked up to the car and punched a hole through the windshield, trying to take my head off. It was like a scene from an action movie. Afterward, he had a big piece of glass hanging out his arm, and we had to rush him to the hospital. Once again, the fault landed on me.

Even when I started rapping, he still didn't believe my future would be prosperous. In fact, no one did except me. He ridiculed me so much, making comments like "You keep on the path you're on and you'll be sitting in Angola with Trell."

As time passed, things began to change for the better and we became closer. When my career began to take off, I decided to make him my manager. After all, he is smart, determined, and, most off all, he is my brother.

Where I'm from, we live by a code: "Keep the money in the family." That's the reason I made my brother my manager. We have had many disagreements and have even argued at times, but it didn't outweigh the good times. Taquari would always tell me I needed to pay attention and listen and stop hearing only what I wanted to hear. That's what I like about him: he doesn't sugarcoat anything. He stays in his own lane and drives it well.

To this day, I still consider us to be like night and day. I have eight children, and he only has one, whom he named Madison Hatch.

This beautiful niece has grown to be one of the smartest little girls I've ever seen. My brother treats her like a queen. I guess you can say that our trials and tribulations as children are what connect us as men. Once he took my side, he's been there ever since.

I try to look beyond our past because to me it was just a learning experience. You know the saying: "You give a little, you take a little." Even through the chaos, my brother has turned out to be an excellent person and one hell of a businessman. That dude right there, he knows how to go get that check. It's just what he does, and he has a way with words. He's the one who shakes hands and negotiates deals, plus he's cold with computers. That alone lets you know who's the brains of the operation. I mean, I'm the brains too, but he's a few levels above me. Oh, as for my real title? I'm the check, not to mention the muscle.

Since we are brothers, I figured we might as well get this money together. I'd cut him in on a nice percentage and we'd both eat. I would finally have someone I could trust, and he'd finally embrace my lifestyle because he was being paid to.

Then one day I ran into some difficulties with my bank account. A situation came about where somehow Taquari was implicated in an incident. This led to the police coming to pick him up. When I heard about it, I had mixed thoughts—I was wigging out for real. I mean, that was my brother we were talking about.

Apparently, some money was taken from my account. Taquari was the only other person who had access. They tried to pin it on him, saying he was involved. I was thinking, *Naw, not my brother. He don't even rock like that.* I wasn't accepting it, but the way they were pushing the issue was like they had solid proof. It was crazy, because after all the years we'd put into building this relationship, that one incident was about to bring it all crumbling down. Eventually, the charges were dropped and they backed off temporarily. Even after he was cleared, the detectives still threw curveballs. It was a bunch of mess. My account took a hit, and it put a huge dent in our relationship.

Turns out there was a ring of people involved. In the group of people was a couple from Cleveland, Ohio, a woman in our extended family. I mean, it was bananas. The sad part about the whole situation was that I lost $469,000 to this mess, and I still haven't been reimbursed for my money. Actually, I'm still fighting for it. The people who did it haven't pled guilty. Come to think of it, they have federal charges behind their actions. I mean they were getting busy out there. They had AK-47s with their names on them and all types of shit. They were draining people's accounts without prejudice.

I can still hear my brother's voice saying, "I didn't do it! I swear to God, I didn't do what they're saying! I wouldn't stoop to anything as low as that, and you know that! You know me, man!"

Taquari and I haven't spoken since that situation because so much shit went bad. We do text one another from time to time. I felt so bad about the shit. I had to text him and let him know that he's bone of my bone and flesh of my flesh, and that I love him more than I can explain. I don't know if it meant anything to him because yet and still, we continue to text only. I can understand, being we're still trying to figure things out.

My momma took his side from the jump. I understand that as well; that's just the way she is. She doesn't speak on it much, but when she does try to slide the topic into the conversation, I use every tactic to duck it. I'm still trying to see what it's gonna be.

Although Taquari and I are only at the level of texting, he does still handle my affairs. He's managing my artist Yung Bleu. I wouldn't take that from him. I just need us to be back in alignment.

Chapter 6

PARENTAL DISCRETION

I know our mother loved us unconditionally. We were made to attend church every Sunday, regardless of what was going on. Choir rehearsal and Bible study were a must in our family. She was deep in her kids' lives. I played basketball, and every game I played, she was there in attendance. Parent-teacher conferences and any programs I got involved in during school, she made it her business to support me and show up. She had one goal in life and she would express it frequently: "to get my family out the hood."

I know she always thought teaching would be what made that dream come true. She loved what she did, and even more so working with the problem kids who had troubled lives and various learning disabilities. She taught at a few different schools—St. Francis Xavier Catholic School, Eden Park Elementary, Dalton Elementary, University

Terrace Elementary, Capitol Elementary, Park Elementary—and she gave her time off to a host of summer programs. She's dedicated more than thirty years to the teaching field, and she's currently the dean of students at Park Elementary. Her commitment level was extremely high and she would tell us in a minute, "I work hard so my kids can have things."

During those years, my father Ray had a drug problem that caused a lot of friction in our home. He was violent and abusive, traits a lot of junkies share. He mostly channeled his attitude toward the Bible-reading Connie. It was as if when he heard her read from the Book he felt like she was casting his demons away. Instead of embracing those words, he'd go crazy and want to fight. When Ray would hit my mother, I would try with all my might to give him a taste of his own medicine, which was impossible because of my size. I was just too scrawny and frail to cause him any harm. He would reach back and slap me, and I would know what pain was.

Sometimes I reflect back on the popular phrase that "God don't like ugly." Maybe as ugly as my father was to his family was the reason God removed him from this life. His death did something to our family, though. Even if it wasn't always peaches and cream when he was around, he was still Momma's husband and our father. I began to become a rebellious young adult. Nothing meant shit to me anymore, not even my love for basketball. It was 1997 when Ray Hatch was called home. My mother was heartbroken. After all he had put her through, she still asked God, "Why?"

I started my rebellious ways and not a soul could tell me I wasn't doing right. I began to steal Momma's car to run the streets and meet with girls. Other nights, when I didn't have her car, she would scour the streets of the hood searching for me. I knew in my heart she just wanted to keep me safe. That is what a mother's love is all about, keeping her children safe. School meant little, if anything, to me. I stayed suspended and in some type of trouble. She preached over and over to me: "Boosie, trouble is easy to get into, but hard to get out of." I didn't comprehend much of that talk then. Later down the line, I wished I had understood what she meant.

Despite Raymond Hatch's problems, I have to say that he was a cool dude at times. The women loved him and thought he was a fine man. I'm glad I took after him physically. I used to love when he got dressed to the nines. He would put on a fly outfit and dapper himself in his chains. I was hard on my daddy, thinking he was gone too much. As I got older, I started to view things as a man walking in his shoes. The lifestyle he'd adopted required him to be in the streets. He couldn't make his money sitting around listening to my mother quote the Bible. I listened to him say on multiple occasions that he couldn't be home and at the same time get money for the house. No kid would understand this coming from his father.

Because I was so young, it made the abuse to Connie seem even worse. He would grab her face, or push her head, or something. As I got older, I tried to see things from his point of view, giving him some benefit of the doubt. I took away that men can't always take all the shit that women say to them.

When Daddy was using, there were times when he was dead wrong. Before he left the house, he would know there was money around—and when he returned high, he would be looking to get it. Raymond would lose it when my mother told him she'd used the money to pay a bill. Those were bad times. I knew it was the drugs that had altered his thinking.

Raymond was talented with his hands. He built out a whole house from our one-bedroom home, adding a kitchen and a living room by himself. He also laid concrete. When I was eleven, he built a Jacuzzi in our yard that held up to ten people. Our home quickly became the place to be.

My daddy did his best, trying to take part in raising us. He just had vices that kept him from being all he could be. As far as the material things, which were the things a lot of fathers think their kids are interested in, he was one hundred percent on top of that. Bikes and clothes, we had because of him. He always said that when he was a kid, his father had kept him fresh, so he would keep his kids fresh the same way. My daddy based a lot of his principles for raising us on the standards he had been raised by. If he was here today, I don't have a clue what I would say to him. I just know I wish he was around. I don't know how to die, but I know I miss the hell out of my father.

Chapter 7
FINDING MYSELF

During first and second grade, I fell sort of in between categories—smart, but bad as ever. I felt it was only fair to exercise my freedom of speech, so I was active, talkative, and a bit of a class clown. I just couldn't stay out of trouble. I'm guessing my actions stemmed from me feeling like I had some kind of leverage, being that my mother was a teacher at the school I attended.

Now, middle school was a bit different. I still had my thuggish ways, I was just more into sports, especially basketball. That was something I was really good at. I'm not talking about the basics, either—I was the starting point guard every year. If I hadn't had to preserve my strength, the coach probably would have kept me in the whole game.

When we'd make our way to the gym before game time, my objective was to show up and show out. The way I controlled that ball,

I thought I was Jordan. The court was my territory; it was where I felt safe. When I was on that blacktop, the only things that mattered were the rim in front of me and the sound of that buzzer.

Those moments kept the sparkle in Momma's eyes. She was really proud of me. She had faith that I had been granted the ability to go pro. She convinced me to play AAU basketball, which had me traveling all over the place.

I have to say, playing sports had its advantages. One thing I realized was women love a superstar. The way they used to scream my name from the bleachers had me going crazy on the courts, and it turned me into a ball hog at times as well. The coach, knowing the deal, would notice and have to pull me out a few times to give me a reality check. That would only last for a few minutes, though. Like I said, I was the star of the team and my presence on the floor was mandatory.

To me, basketball was like a good song. You know, when you're at a party and a good song comes on? Everybody gets up and starts dancing. Then once the song stops, so does the dancing. But a good song and the artist who made it will stay in the conversation long after. In basketball, the screaming and cheering goes on throughout the game, and it all stops once the game ends. But a good game, and the star player's name, will stay in rotation long after the final buzzer.

I had women approach me from out of nowhere, throwing themselves on me. They would even do this alongside the other women who were with them. Chicks used to follow me home just to see where I was living. I mean, my sex game was at an all-time high.

During those times, it would have been ridiculous for me to even think about commitment. Don't get me wrong, the thought will cross a young player's mind—hell, some might even go as far as trying it. I'm not saying all ballplayers should always be single. What I am saying is, stay away from strays and loose ends. Where I'm from, we define loose ends as women—with or without kids—who are going through difficult times, due to a lack of willingness to do better for themselves. Women can be the biggest deceivers, especially the ones trying to eat through a niggah's bank account.

Other than that, my high school years were some of the best years of my life. I was a bit of a geek in Social Studies. Some people called me the gardener because I was constantly digging up my roots. That's just how I was, searching for those footprints that cleared the way. I was always moved by those who, as Jeezy would say it, put on for their city—whatever form that might take. These were the men who put others before themselves. People like Martin Luther King Jr., Malcolm X, and Pastor Jimmy Swaggart, these were my heroes.

Some people might question that last one, but I couldn't care less about what anyone has to say about him. That man has done more for Baton Rouge than the government. That man put himself and his career on the line to help us. He was that mentor, father figure, and big brother most of us needed. I remember him coming through the hood to feed those who were less fortunate. Every weekend, he'd come and take us places. Whether he took us to the movies, out to eat, or shopping, he was there for us kids. He was a ghetto superhero.

Chapter 8

PRODUCT OF MY ENVIRONMENT

allowed myself to become a victim of my circumstances. My yearning for that which I lacked inspired me to reach for that which I could obtain—illegally, of course, but at a much faster pace.

Being born in the ghetto, it was what I knew. The ghetto is my home. It carried me all those years, and it endured all the damage I did to the block. When you live in the ghetto, you know firsthand about the killings, the drug raids, and the robberies. You know about the Amber Alerts and the abductions, because you're right there in the circle of everything that connects.

After school, I got deep up in the streets. Cocaine was the trail of bread crumbs that led the way out. That's all we were searching for—an exit. So, yeah, I chose that path. Drugs have always been a part of my life. I mean, like, since forever. That's the devil of all devils.

I couldn't believe the damage it caused my family. You'd think Hurricane Katrina was involved the way it tore through our bloodline. Mainly because my father had been a member of *Star Trek* since the beginning, doing anything he could do to get that high, even if it meant crossing his own. I was young, but I knew, and it was the one thing I knew for sure. I knew about drugs before they knew about me.

My neighborhood was an outlet to it all. I mean, marijuana, cocaine, heroin, angel dust—a one-stop shop. You name it and it was there for the taking, and if not, it was only a phone call away. The demand for cocaine made it the drug of choice. You were either selling, smoking, or snorting. It was destroying anyone who faced off with it. It didn't matter whether man or woman; they were both taking a beating and it showed in their features.

Some people underestimate the power of cocaine. I watched that stuff rip through my uncle's life, causing him to jeopardize his pro football career. There would have been hope in his future had he chosen a better set of friends. The way I looked at it, coke wasn't the problem. His friends were the problem, because they were the ones pressuring him to buy more and more. That was their only agenda and the only purpose of their presence. It got so bad that eventually he relinquished his Super Bowl ring for a quick fix.

I hated that shit coming up, especially watching it transform my dad, my uncle, and most of their friends as well. It had them really tripping and looking bad. It was in their faces and appearances; it was undeniable. They were all on the same road to destruction. At the end of the day, I knew that shit played a role in Daddy's death.

I had been watching cocaine get bagged, cooked, sold, and snorted since I was a little boy. It wasn't a big deal. Back then, I was just an observer. I didn't know it could make you rich, I just knew it could fuck you up. When I was eight years old, I blazed my first blunt. That shit caught me off guard. I was high as hell and thought I was seeing shit. So, I rejected it—that wasn't my thing. The shit was strong and it was nasty.

But that was then. As I got older, things began changing. I was more into the streets, and weed was something I now desired. I got hooked on marijuana after my pops passed. In the beginning, I tried to hide my addiction, but the more I thought about my pops and the situation my mother was in, the more I smoked. As time passed, it was pretty evident I was a weedhead.

I was moving cocaine and marijuana on a daily basis. I was pushing weed on the hill by Old Man Lehman and Deborah's spot on Garfield Street, near LSU. That's where it was popping the most. Money was flowing through there all day and night. Most of our customers were LSU students. The benefit of their business was that you didn't have to give them much. You could easily bag up two hundred fifty dollars in dime bags and get it off the same day. The college students were sweet. We used to sell them half ounces for the price of ounces. Yeah, the weed was moving. But crack? That was something different. Cross the Tracks, that's where everything was going down. The junkies were moving around like zombies.

I used to sit in front of my grandmother's house and make that paper. I was young, so the money had me tripping. It got to the point that I didn't care who I sold it to. I was selling to my uncle, his people, and a few other relatives of mine. Ironic, isn't it? The thing I once resented, I was now pushing through my bloodline. At that point, it was whatever to me. I'm talking I was straight 'bout it, by any means, anything it took to get paid. That's how it was across the tracks. Anybody could get it, family or not. If you were smoking it, we were selling it to you. I could see the effects it could have on the strongest person, so using was never an option for me personally.

At the age of seventeen, I met the plug I'd been looking for. I called him Dig. He took a liking to me as soon as we met. Apparently, he was liking the way I was moving. Every time I made enough to re-up, I'd hit his line. I didn't wait until I sold out; I got right to the money. After a month or so, the plug was calling me. We used to hang out and just shoot the shit. He even started allowing me to use his car. I would have it for weeks, sometimes months, on end. Every week, he was flooding me with coke and weed. It got to the point I didn't have to spend my money anymore. Hell, he wouldn't accept it. From that point on, I had become a loading dock and all I was seeing was profit.

Every week, I was getting a package of five pounds and a four-and-a-split. I was moving that shit like clockwork. Life was looking up for me. I mean, shit was so good that I ended up dropping out of school. I was doing way too much and the cops were always chasing me, so school was just a dead zone. I felt like with the money I was making from hustling and rapping, I didn't need school.

All my life I'd been observing hustlers and how they operated. I was putting the pieces together, creating my own blueprint. I was ambitious, determined, and unlike many others, willing to accept the downside of the game.

I would use the mind skill which I'd gotten from Calvin Ricks, a man the streets honored and respected. This man was a mastermind, a pure genius. He was a jack-of-all-trades. Ricks had a way about him that most dudes couldn't comprehend. Let's take the game, for instance. While most dealers were disrespectful and flat-out heartless to the customers, Ricks would treat them with respect. When they approached him looking like a mummy, wrapped in dirty clothing, barely breathing, he still treated them like a person.

He was the type to give you a blanket or something to eat before you left. He knew that no matter how a person appeared at that moment, there was always a past behind them. Ricks looked at them for what they were: human. For that mindset alone all the addicts loved him and wouldn't dare to shop elsewhere.

The man was an icon, so for that reason I studied him like a math problem. I took my A in the game once I got up in his business. He showed me the ropes, and I hung on to every sentence for survival tactics. I admired the way he could talk to you and change your whole way of thinking for the better. He was a motivator, the type of person who'd build you up. He saw the potential in others.

■ ■ ■

You have to be careful in the game because minor mistakes can cost you or those around you. That's what happened to me.

It was eighty degrees out and the block was pumping. The way the hood was packed with customers kind of made me feel like I was in New York. Shit was sweet, but the cops had their own agenda.

Like any other day, we were out blazing blunts and popping bottles while tending to the business. Out of nowhere cops swept through the hood in unmarked cars and trucks and shit. Hell, they even came through in a fire truck and an ambulance. They blocked us in like sitting ducks to the point there was nothing we could do. We couldn't believe those bitches came with such force. I know one thing that was certain about that day: my man Rome wasn't going. Strapped and never questioning death, he drew his weapon in an attempt to make a statement. When I looked into his eyes I immediately took cover. Rome was maybe able to get off one shot before they plugged him. The way his body took those bullets, there was no way he could survive. As his body hit the ground, his eyes were fixed on me. We all ended up going to jail that night. They had me marinating in the County for a few days while the murder was under investigation.

While I was confined, being famous kept me socializing, and that's where I was introduced to my second plug. The niggah had some interesting things about him, but at the same time he ran his mouth. We exchanged info, but that's as far as it got just then.

■ ■ ■

After I was released I got back to business. The crazy thing is that I ended up bumping heads with that plug about a year later. I didn't even notice him at first, but he spotted me instantly. Less than a minute into the conversation it dawned to me: *Oh, this the niggah I met in the County on some funny-type shit.* Our first conversation led me to believe that he was a pimp, but we eventually got to it.

Now that we were out and back on the streets, the conversation was a bit different. At that point real numbers came into play. After he gave me full insight on who he was and what he had access to, I couldn't believe the age he was drafting his pounds at. The shit was a few hundred dollars less than what I was paying already. It sounded too sweet to be true. At first I thought he was a fed, until the streets said different. We exchanged numbers and talked a little more. The first time we did business was the first time I ever saw a bale of marijuana. It was a rectangular block that looked like three couches put together. *Holy shit!* was all I could think. *It's about to go down.*

Showing up in the hood with something like that, I was deemed to be the man. I felt there was nothing better in life than to become the hood distributor. I was now able to set everybody straight.

At nineteen years old, I was paid and living damn good. I had my own apartment, two cars, and my daughter didn't need anything. I did try to go back to McKinley High School. That lasted about seven to eight months before I ended up quitting again. That same year,

I was introduced to something new on the market. They called it ecstasy. It was a big thing too. I was the last one from the hood to try it. My older cousins had been on it for about a year at that time. Eventually, they influenced most of our friends to try it. I couldn't knock them; I just thought it wasn't for me. My thing was smoking and drinking daiquiris.

I remember back when I copped my candy-black old-school Monte Carlo. It was equipped with twenty-inch Daytons, two TVs, a touch-screen CD player, and four twelve-inch subwoofers. We ain't gonna even talk about the paint job. It was so clean, it was like a mirror. When I drove down the street, all eyes were on my fly ride. I had copped it from this guy named KK out of Glen Oaks. He was known for some of the coldest old-school whips cruising the streets.

I can remember that day because I was baited in to pop a pill. My people were trying to get me to go out. What better way to step out than being lit? By the time we got to the Matrix in Uptown, I was rolling and that was without the wheels. I felt like a young Gotti. Those pills gave me a feeling I will never forget, reason being I was hooked instantly. The shit made me feel special. I felt more loved. I mean, I would pop a pill and fuck my girl like I was Congo or something. The next morning, she would look at me and be like, "You all right? You fucked me last night like you just got out of prison." That shit just made me laugh.

From 2000 through 2002, everybody was popping pills. Men and women, I mean, everybody. It got so heavy that Baton Rouge was nicknamed Jigga City. In 2001, I was introduced to syrup. Syrup is promethazine and codeine. This guy from Uptown named Delmis turned me on to my first purple Sprite. We hung out all that day, and when he dropped me off, he handed me a blunt and a two-liter Sprite with an ounce of cough syrup mixed in it. The shit was excellent, and the taste of it made you drink it like Kool-Aid. From that day on, I was a junkie.

I'm a thinker, so I always had something brewing in my mind. I had a plan. I started putting everybody in the hood up on syrup. Not long after, everybody was sipping. I had pill poppers wanting to sip until they drank more than they popped pills. It gives you this drowsy feeling; that's why they call it "lean."

Soon I ended up getting this sweet-ass plug on the drank. With that, I had the streets on lock. If anybody was copping lean, nine times out of ten they were getting it from me. Remember I told you I had copped that crucial plug? He was from New Orleans and he never ran out of drank. Believe me when I tell you the money was plentiful. I was selling about a hundred pints every twenty-four to forty-eight hours. My plug was amazed when he saw how the money was moving. I had that shit moving like crack, I mean all the way from Baton Rouge to Mississippi, even down to Alabama.

I remember one time I was on my way back from picking up a package and I had to piss really badly because I was full of the drank. I ended up having to pull over on the highway. I was in my 745, as conspicuous as a billboard on the side of the road. Suddenly a state trooper pulled up behind me. In the trunk, I had a hundred pints of cough syrup. I could tell he was on some bullshit—a young Black man driving a fifty-thousand-dollar car, I'm sure that didn't sit right with him. If he'd found that drank, it would be curtains.

He exited the vehicle, his hand resting on his weapon. When I glanced down at his holster, I noticed he'd already removed the safety strap. I had taken precautions and left my gun at home in case something like this happened, but the look in his eyes made me question that decision. As he approached, he inquired why I had pulled over. I quickly gave him a spiel about checking my tires. I told him one had felt kind of low while I was driving, so I'd wanted to check it to make sure there weren't any hazards.

By pure luck, there was a call over the radio that caught his attention. Man, you don't understand when I tell you that my heart was beating like a drumroll. All I could do was thank the Lord for his deliverance. It was crazy, all he did was tell me to have a nice day. Before he was out of earshot, he actually looked back and complimented my ride, saying I had a nice car. It was a close call that day on I-10.

As time passed I continued doing my thing. I was drinking so much that I would get sick and could barely even shit. I'd really started drinking to get off the pills. The shit worked, but the drank had my body in even worse condition than the pills had. Business was still booming. Not only was I selling drank, I was still selling coke and weed as well. People had mad trust in me, so they were giving me plenty of coke to sell. I'd get it off quick and return their take, and the rest was all profit to me. I mean, even though I was rapping, hustling was my heart. The way I did it made me think it was a gift. Anything I'd put my hands on would disappear. I made niggaz into incredibly good hustlers. I was turning little boys into grown men. Deadbeats were turning into real fathers. Those who lacked were hurting for nothing. I mean, I can actually say I made a lot of people want more out of life.

I wasn't the type of hustler to reject a niggah just because he came from a different hood. Naw, not me. I wasn't turning down shit but my collar. Never would I allow my feelings to overshadow my hustle. I think I got that from Ricks. The only thing that got in the way of that was my music. At one point, I had to push away from hustling because it was interfering with my career. That's when the money was flowing like water, and I was thirsty. I figured I'd be stupid to keep hustling when I was bringing in the same amount of money off a show. Why score a brick when I could just do a show and make the same amount?

By hustling so hard and thinking of ways to capture these streets, it would take my mind off my dream, even though that life gave me a lot to rap about. If I could, I'd take it back, believe me I would, and focus on the gift God had given me. That would be my wish. Also, it would take away some of the envy of the haters out here. Like the ones who killed my main man, Lil Ivy. Still to this day, I regret not being there. Muthafuckas caught my man slipping with his pants down. I guess they say it comes with the territory. That's the thing about this dope game: the many things obtained can easily be taken away.

I loved being a doe boy. My objectives in the game were to outshine everyone and fuck as many women as possible. During my teen years, which to me seemed to be the years with the most value, I stayed knocking something down, and of course at that time I was off weed and lean.

During those times, I was taking in three to four women a day. The pills gave me all the energy I needed and gave me a sense of cockiness. I would see two females digging me and I'd inquire if I could have them both. Eighty percent of the time it was a go. I was the man. My name stayed in the bright lights. I owned the streets and the music game. Jealousy was brewing everywhere. Niggaz was giving me looks of envy. And of course there's always a knucklehead thinking his shit don't stank.

Word got back to me that these niggaz across the tracks were plotting my demise. The shit had me bitter, knowing all the love I'd given to these streets over the years. Yet envy and hatred overshadowed my kindness. Once again it was time to show niggaz I was more than just a stage performer.

We couldn't be half-assed because them niggaz across the tracks had obtained the same street credibility as my crew and me. When we took it to them, we had to be discreet. They were a gang of young niggaz, corrupt in every aspect. They were making a lot of noise out there in the open, but my clique and I were about to quiet that down. They were known for their gritty tactics and connections with the law.

Once the plan was put into effect, I immediately gave my seal of approval. The only thing left was to wait for nightfall. Wearing all-black hoodies and ski masks, we camped out in the bushes, waiting for them to make their move. We put a little young niggah on the corner with a chirp to warn us of any sightings. The moon was out. Then one of the homies gave a whistle, giving us a heads-up.

An all-black Audi hit the corner. The paint job was so wet that you'd swear you were standing next to a mirror. The windows were tinted, making it impossible to see inside. None of that mattered though; no one was walking away alive that night. We positioned ourselves, clutching our weapons, ready to go out in a blaze of glory if need be.

To our surprise, another car hit the corner only seconds later. Either they were together or the second vehicle was on what we were on. Fuck it! Everyone could get it. With guns aimed in their direction, we prepared to fire . . . until the second car turned on its flashers.

"Oh shit, it's the cops!" my niggah Shooney said as he stuffed his gun in his waistband.

We all did the same as we quickly vacated the premises. All I could think was that God looks out for babies and fools. We considered that as a warning sign and disappeared into the night.

Chapter 9

THE TRANSITION

I've always been a boss.

My love of music started when I was small. My mother always had something around the house jammin' while she did her thing. If she was cooking, she played certain music; if she was cleaning, she had a custom selection for that as well. I could hear a song on the radio and remember the lyrics instantly. To me, it was like a gift. I remember being a die-hard fan of the groups Jodeci, N.W.A, Geto Boys, and a few others, like Pac of course and Slick Rick. I even loved R. Kelly's music.

When I was like eight or nine, you could hear me all the time rapping the music I heard, going word for word along with the artist. My uncle used to joke that when I was a shorty, even the first words he heard me say sounded like a rap. At the age of eleven I elevated my skills and started freestyling about things I'd seen or heard. I would only display those skills for my close friends and family, because at that age, it wasn't yet my dream to become a big rap star. My friends would try to get me to flow, but I had to be in the mood to do it. As I grew older, my skills grew and I really became good at it. Still, I didn't ever think I would become a rap star.

I did my first rap performance at my high school in ninth grade at the Southern Battle of the Bands. The high school band played the beat, and I came out and rapped over their sound. To me, that was my first taste of getting rap fame. After that show, it had me growing more attached to the art form. Previously, basketball had been my first love and dream. I think every kid wanted to be the next Magic Johnson or Michael Jordan. But the response from the other students alerted me that I had serious rapping talent.

I was doing a song every day, putting together rhymes. I wanted to make people eventually notice that I had a real talent for this rap game. One or two years passed, and I was writing raps all the time. Soon, I had several notebooks full of songs I had penned. Only a few close friends knew about the collection I had managed to put together: Head Busser, Karly, John, Marcus, Corey, Chug, and Kirby. Nobody in the hood could out-rap me. I had a song for any situation.

My dreams started to shift from the ball court to the studio. When my daddy passed, it made me want to get into a studio even more. My cousins all knew I could go on the mic, but they didn't know how good I had become. They wanted to hear me all the time, but I would change the subject. After losing my father, I really had to be in the mood. One night I had gotten drunk and one of my cousins and Ed Lover were there. I rapped all night long, rap after rap, I just kept flowing. That was the night they started drilling in my head that I was destined to do this—that I was meant to be a big-time rap star.

"Lil niggah, listen. All the shit you've been through, you have a story to tell," they said, and it made me think. "You could be getting paid," they continued. My cousins had some serious connections in the streets because they were gangstas. That was how I got connected to Frog, through my cousins. Frog was a G from the hood known as the plug. He was connected with a niggah named C-Loc who was really doing his thing.

C-Loc was partners with another dude named Young Bleed, and together they had what was called Concentration Camp. C-Loc was also connected to Master P, and Concentration Camp was part of the big song "How Ya Do Dat." Everybody in the South and even other parts of the world was bumping this track. C-Loc came on the block one day, probably because my cousin had summoned him. Back in the day when you had real homies, they would come when you called, no question.

I was shooting the ball in the gym when C-Loc and Frog walked in and called me outside. Frog looked me in the eye and I knew he was all about his business. "Let me see what you got, lil niggah," he said. I remember not even being nervous. I knew one thing for sure: this was my chance to prove what I had.

I spat like never before, watching C-Loc's reaction to what he was hearing. I couldn't tell what he was thinking, but it became obvious when I finished and he told me to get in the van—I was heading straight to the studio. I was only like fifteen at the time, but I was street savvy. C-Loc was all business. My mind was racing in a thousand different directions when we entered the studio. I first thought that since I had the words and they had the music, once the music came on, my words would fit with any beat. But I had some problems at first because that wasn't the way it worked. You can't just rap to a beat with your premade lyrics and expect it to fit. I had to learn how to ride the beats, and once that part of it came to me, I had it. People in the studio were amazed at my delivery.

The studio was cool, but I was still making more money hanging in the hood, doing my thing. C-Loc had to find a way to keep me off the corners long enough to do the music. I wasn't realizing at first the magnitude of how rapping could really change my life. I wanted that fast, right-now currency. The corners were paying me and allowed me and my crew to stay fresh so we could go clubbing and show off for the ladies. Fly gear and fat pockets got you girls; they were loving us. We would pack into my Monte Carlo, fresh to death, and wreak havoc on the club scene.

C-Loc continued to be on me, dragging me to the studio and polishing my talent, until I honed in on what I was really capable of. The first song C-Loc and I recorded was "Shit Real." We were suitable to each other's flow and we made good music. When we did "Outlaws," that song caught the attention of a lot of ears, and I began getting hotter by the second. Also my song "That's My Thug There" had caught some major attention and was becoming a rap classic. My verse was so heartfelt and real that people had to respect the lyrics. It was like I had come out of nowhere and earned the label "hard-hitter" in the camp.

I had South Baton Rouge and Fieldtown on lock. Everywhere you went they were playing Boosie music. On every corner and in every car that had booming systems, you heard my flow coming from their speakers. People were talking about every song I laid a verse on, especially the joint "Nice Action," which also became a hood classic. My buzz grew quickly and we decided it was time for me to finally drop an album.

My first album was actually forced on me. I had everything I needed in me except for the discipline to complete something. I think C-Loc was fed up with me pussyfooting around. He was a businessman and he had come up with a plan. That was when he got me, Lil E, and JR in his van and just drove off, heading for Texas. C-Loc's intelligence told him Baton Rouge was a bad distraction for me, and instead of doing what I was supposed to be doing, I would be chasing the wrong type of currency. He was right because my block was rolling super-hard and it was an everyday payday if you were on those corners. I was making a couple of dollars doing shows, but when I got that money, my head was on flipping it.

Once we arrived in Texas, we first hit the mall and I did some extravagant shopping, all on his dime. After that, it was business as usual. We hit the studio and I was forced to record my first album. I was told in a nice, sincere way that I wasn't leaving until the work was completed.

It was a lot of work, and I couldn't see the bigger picture at the time. Music wasn't really paying me enough to give too much time producing it. But they had everything laid out for me, including my weed. That was the relaxation I needed to do what I had to. I was the youngest on the team, and it didn't take long for my style to capture a big audience. I was instantly hot in the South—Mississippi, Alabama, and of course my hometown—the people were loving me.

Three months after the first day in Texas, I dropped my first solo album, titled *Youngest of da Camp*. That first drop got me mad respect in the streets, but as we all know, along with respect comes the haters. Everywhere you turned, those tracks were ringing out like it was the only rap album out at the time. I was getting congrats from people all over. They were strung out on "That Night," "Feel Lucky," "Same Ol Shit," and "My Life." The disc was so hot even the intros became classics. I was now doing shows all over Louisiana, Mississippi, and Alabama.

My head exploded, and at that point it was time to drop out of school. I felt I could put it on hold because I was too big for the teachers to teach. I was now a rapper, a student of a different game. I was about to be well known for doing the same thing as Pac was doing. I looked up to him, and to be able to do what he was doing was where it was. I'm not glorifying any kid dropping out of school. I know for a fact that not every person with talent will make it to the big leagues. It doesn't matter if you're a ballplayer, track star, or rapper, school is something we all need. I dropped out and tried to go back from time to time, but I wasn't really for the lessons the teachers were giving. Like I said, I made a few bad choices in life, but everyone's choices define them at some point. Sometimes bad choices work out for the better; sometimes they end up giving you a life you never would have dreamed of.

When I went back in twelfth grade, school was different than when I'd left. They even had state troopers at the building, and they wouldn't let the students park their whips in front. I was tripping because I was only there to show out. I had my fly-ass Monte Carlo on twenty-twos, laced with TVs everywhere, and another fly ride. I wanted to be seen and heard. To me, school had become a hassle, and that's what helped me make my final decision to leave. I would still ride up on Fridays, because the football games were live and I didn't want to miss the chance to be seen.

The first time I got in trouble at the schoolhouse and got a two-day detention was when I was trying to holla at this little niggah who was about his paper. Dude hit me to give me seventeen pounds of weed and my mindset was I wanted to fuck with it. I wanted the product, but I really wanted to get in this little niggah's good graces. He was the plug on the weed at the time, and I had heard nothing but good things about his business practices. I left school, went and made my play, and came back.

When I got back, somebody had snitched on me. I never found out who, but I didn't care; I wasn't at school to learn. I was strictly showing off the new person I was and trying to get at every girl I could. At that age, when you're fresh every day, with clothes, money, and cars, you can get almost any girl. They really want to be with the freshest niggah so they can show off, just like that man is doing.

I recall some baller-ass shit I used to do every lunch period. I know people say the way to a man's heart is through his stomach. Well, I learned the way to get to a girl's panties was the exact same. I ordered boxes of pizzas every day so the girls could eat free. I let my niggahs eat too, but that was a player move to get the attention from the girls. When are you doing stuff like that, everyone in the building is going to take notice of you. You become the man, even to your haters.

Always with urban fame comes the urban dilemmas. A month after the CD dropped, my CEO C-Loc got into an altercation with J-Tweezy and was sentenced to a few years in prison. I was hurting because I truly knew there was no one else who could run the label like C-Loc. His tutelage was what kept me grounded. He did the beats, set up the shows, and called all the shots. It was like . . . what would the *Sopranos* be without Tony? That's what I was up against now that he was gone.

There was one thing I knew I could turn to: the block. I went right back there, getting money in the streets. My drive for the music was slipping away. I had a feeling that with C-Loc out the picture, I was going to be a one-album wonder, like many who had come and then faded away.

With all that had transpired, I felt this was my second chance at doing this thing on another level, and I started recording right away. It was going to be a great joint, full of banging tracks. Somehow everything got leaked, which put a damper on things, so I started working on another album. In another thirty days, I was ready to drop my second solo project, *For My Thugz*. When that album hit the streets, it was popping harder than the first joint. It ripped through the South like a hurricane as it tore up the airwaves and sound systems. With tracks like "Wonder Why Your Child So Bad" and "Consequences," the whole playlist was classics. I was now seen as a god in my city and my come-up was inevitable. That still didn't stop me from going hard on the streets. I wasn't quite drawn out of the fast life just yet.

Shows started bringing in real money, and my name was becoming household news around the country. That was when Lil Webbie came and we dropped the classic duo album *Ghetto Stories*. The combination of the two of us working together hit the streets like an earthquake. Everybody was feeling that joint. I had women by the boatload coming for me after that project. Just like me, Webbie was spitting that gangsta shit, so we couldn't be anything but lethal. The streets were feeling us so hard that we came back the following year with *Gangsta Musik*. That CD was like a new version of a crack epidemic—everybody had to have it. We were killing it with radio playtime, and not only that, shows started being booked across the country, coast to coast.

Suddenly, other rap artists were making contact weekly, calling for features. I was hot, and every track I put a verse on blew up. "I Smoke, I Drank" blew the fuck up, "Do tha Ratchet" blew the fuck up, and "Beast Mode" went hard as hell and blew the fuck up. Like with every relationship, Webbie and I had our disagreements—but we were like blood brothers. Brothers fight and then hug the next day. That was our relationship.

Once word hit, major labels started calling. We received a deal, which in turn allowed our product to get distributed nationwide. Even so, we were told we had to sell records before we would see the real paper. I remember when Trill signed the distribution deal, Webbie and I both were on the radio stunting like we were rich, but we didn't get the check. We were lying, but I was happy that our music was now going to be nationwide and we were going to be on television making videos and doing interviews.

I wasn't tripping too hard at the moment because I was still eating from the streets and the shows I was doing. I was dropping mixtapes constantly and was also getting those paydays. But there was something about that game money that I loved. Maybe it was the fact that the game money all was mine; nobody had a hand in my pocket when it came to that money.

My first video was with David Banner and Magic on a joint called "Ain't Got Nothing." That video made it to BET, which was cool, but deep down in my soul, I knew I wanted my own video. I knew it would come soon. A lot of times artists make it but owe so much on the back end, they are broke before the check reaches them. Everything the label Trill did for us—from hotel rooms to meals—had to be accounted for: it was all written down, and we had to pay every dime of it back. It's almost like fame is fronted to you, something similar to doing business with the cartel families. Webbie and I used to sit back and talk about how we were in debt and owed them, but in the end, we still loved them for the platform and the father-figure lessons they taught us.

Next, Webbie dropped *Savage Life* and I dropped *Bad Azz*. We were now nationally known and getting crazy show money. "Show Money King" was what they called me in the magazines. I was doing it all and it didn't matter to me—shows, birthday parties, clubs, walkthroughs, whatever—I was a hustler. If you had it, I was coming to get it. When the fans screamed my name, the adrenaline rush it gave me was insane. Hearing that made me never want to leave the stage. After I dropped *Bad Azz*, the following year under my own label, Bad Azz Entertainment, I started killing the mixed-tape game. Also I was featured on plenty of number-one hits, like "Out Here Grindin," "Independent," "Hey Bae," and "Everything." I was one of few rappers featured on the multi-platinum-selling album *The Recession*.

When I put my verse on "Wipe Me Down," I was on top of the world; the haters couldn't see me after that. That song was truly a moneymaker, going number one on the charts and also becoming one of the hottest ringtones ever. I can remember back in 2007 I actually performed my verse of "Wipe Me Down" at the BET Awards and stole the show. I figured, for those who didn't know Boosie Badazz before that night, now they did. In 2008, I got a chance to grace the cover of *XXL* magazine, which I was fly as fuck on.

Chapter 10

GANGSTER, GANGSTER

veryone in the ghetto idolizes gangsters at some point. Growing up where I come from, you admired them until you were old enough to become one. Believe me, I was well on my way—the shit was in my blood. No matter what the fuck I did, there was no escaping my fate.

My mother tried her best to keep me away from the drug game, but she had to understand something: you can't walk the devil into church and ask him to pray.

Watching the older cats in my hood when I was coming up, I knew I was amongst the special ranks. Those cats had style, character, and a fuck-the-world attitude that kept their haters hating. They held down the social structure in the hood. Neighbors were considered family and elders were treated with the utmost respect. These heads paid the youngsters to mow grass and run to the store for the old folks and the disabled.

I soon realized that these services were reciprocal. It was an insurance policy and safety net for when the cops invaded the block. The neighborhood would leave their garages open and back doors unlocked, giving the OGs a means of escape from the police. It was brilliant, and I would follow those same guidelines when it was my time.

When I felt I was seasoned enough in the street game to leave the nest, it was with one objective—to be the fuckin' boss. I started on my road to success by applying those moves I'd collected from the OGs. I mounted up a group of guys with the same objectives as I had, and we started our journey.

Like with any business, in the beginning we covered much ground in finding suppliers and customers. In due time, the road smoothed out. We were a new generation, a pack of hungry wolves that needed to be fed. We lived each day like there was no tomorrow, and only time would tell what was to come next.

As things progressed, we found ourselves beefing with other crews on a regular basis. We were ready, though. Whether it was scrapping or pulling out pistols, to us it made no fucking difference. We lived for the day and owned the night. A lot of other cats didn't like that and our manhood was tried constantly. With us being a younger breed, we were forced to prove our worth.

The crazy thing is that most of my encounters came from the older guys. These dudes were already in their late twenties and early thirties, the ones who considered themselves the founders of the game. Back when they were runnin' the block, these same niggaz commended you on your hustle. They facetiously wished you happiness while fearing your rise. I could see through their bullshit.

At one point, I ended up connecting with some cats I assumed to be thorough because they used to run with a few cousins of mine. They saw my shine and would always tell me I was destined to make it. Once I made it, it seemed as though my success hit their funny bones. To some, me winning was no longer a celebration but a stumbling block. Misery loves company, and these dudes were full of it.

One thing I learned was everything that glitters ain't gold. Winning is everything and everyone wants to be a part of it—but just because you look like money doesn't mean you have it. Back then, in my eyes winning was a niggah who could easily obtain ten to twenty thousand without delay. As an upcoming teen, twenty to thirty g's meant you were the man. Poverty was clear and present, so if a niggah was having that type of income, he was king of the hood. Personally, I looked up to those kinds of dudes. That was until I was a click from being twenty—which was when I got my first hundred pack.

I came from nothing, so to me this was making progress. I could easily count on one hand the people in my hood around my age who made that kind of money. Many of the older guys couldn't even keep up. I was a problem for some, but I expected that, so it didn't bother me.

I was moving up in the game. My brother used to tell me I was speed-racing and needed to tap the brake a bit. I knew he meant well, but the lane I'd chosen wouldn't allow it. Even if I'd wanted to slow down, I don't believe I could have.

With all the weed, pills, and lean I had consumed, I felt like a passenger and the substances had control of the vehicle. Given the opportunity to step outside of myself if only for a second, maybe my reactions to certain situations would have been handled differently. Perhaps my journey could have taken an entirely different turn. Who knows, being that those times are now lost. Once they're gone, we can never get them back.

Every now and then, my brother's words of advice would cross my mind. Looking in the mirror daily, I had to be honest with myself and admit that despite our differences, my brother was right. There were those moments I felt like just relinquishing it all. Hell, I was tired. Not sleepy—more like worn out and fucking exhausted. Tired of the bullshit, tired of trying to meet the expectations of everyone around me, and tired of these cutthroat niggaz and money-hungry bitches counting my pockets.

Oh, and we're not going to leave out those crooked-ass police who continued to harass and extort me. This is the fucking law I'm talking about, the ones sworn to protect and serve. How the hell are they protecting us when they're killing us and getting away with it? Sometimes your brain, body, and spirit need to disassociate to regain stability. Life will take you like a hurricane if you aren't holding on to the important things.

I thought it was about being a boss. But in all actuality, it was about surviving. It was about being blessed with time in this life. I realized that the more I put into my hustle, the more I was lowering my chances for survival. I had to look at the bigger picture, which was my children. They mean the world to me, so much that I would sacrifice my life to benefit theirs.

My eyes have seen a lot of things, the type of shit people usually get murdered for. With all the bullshit I've done, seen, or been part of, I have often wondered: *When the fuck is it my time? Is God fucking with me? Is He saving me for last? What's this Niggah's agenda? Am I meant to suffer while watching those around me die?* It was chaotic.

I remember one day we were leaving the house and we were about twenty deep. There was so much beef and drama surrounding us that we had to be deep like that. I was the man, so people were trying their best to get at me. No matter how much love I showed these streets, it still went unappreciated. The day was beautiful, so we knew plenty of bitches would be out. Everyone was outside enjoying the weather. Only a fool would be stuck in the house. Barbeque grills were smoking, loud music was playing, and the little girls in the neighborhood were out playing double Dutch. Yeah, today was going to be a good day. We decided to head to the mall.

When I exited the house, my crew was posted on the porch and around the gate. With things escalating in the hood, my attire now included two chrome-and-black Millennium nine-millimeters and a bulletproof vest. I knew my haters were out lurking, so I had to be prepared. The beef had turned up with those niggaz on the other side of the tracks. From my understanding, some little niggah who went by the name Mouse was calling the shots for them cats. The niggah had allegedly caught two bodies out in Oakland and had come down here to escape murder charges. I guess he'd been here for at least six months, trying to hold things down. From what I was hearing, he was getting money.

Word was he had been sending complaints over my way, saying my people were invading his space. *His space?* I thought to myself. That niggah couldn't be serious! Then he has the audacity to send some little girl over to deliver a message. She handed me a piece of paper which read, "We need to meet to discuss some business arrangements." At the end of the note, in the lower right-hand corner, was a stamp of a mouse. Right then I knew there was going to be a problem with this niggah. My partner didn't take too kindly to it, so he snatched the note from me and wiped his ass with it. He then folded it back up and handed the little girl a hundred dollar bill to return the note to its sender. From that day on, it was all-out warfare.

I won't deny that Mouse was nobody's fool—he really did get down. That made the situation a bit more interesting. We got confirmation that when he received the note, he had been eating lunch. When he opened it, he damn near bumped his head as he fell backwards in his chair. He grabbed the tablecloth and spilled his plate across his chest. He jumped off the floor and searched around for his pistol.

On our way to the mall, this black-on-black Lexus GS hit the corner like a chase scene in a movie. The sound of screeching tires put us on full alert. Some members of my crew found cover before they got the chance to pull their weapons out, while I and a few others were out to connect some dots.

I took aim and gave that fuckin' car everything I had in my clip. It sped by so fast and there were so many innocent bystanders that the crew couldn't light that bitch up the way we wanted. We practically chased them halfway down the block, hoping to get better shots. With three clips in my pockets, I was reloading as I gave chase.

The shit didn't seem right to me. It felt like a scare tactic, and I knew that Mouse was past that amateur shit. I knew how the boy got down, and that shit wasn't his style at all. Something was up, I just didn't know what. The homies were boasting like we'd done something, but I suspected otherwise.

Moments later we learned that car had only been the decoy. While our backs were turned, a second vehicle, an all-black SUV, came out the alley. All the windows were rolled down and guns were pointed out of every one of them, including the driver's.

"Watch out, Boosie!" yelled some of the bystanders.

When I turned to see what the commotion was, all I could see was muzzle flashes coming out the windows of the SUV. I raised my piece for the second time to destroy these niggaz, but before I could, my niggah Backwood was pushing me out the way. That's when he ended up catching one on my behalf. They kept firing on us, some of them even stepping out of the vehicle. Seeing my man on the ground gagging up blood lit a fuse in me. Without thinking, I stood up, again taking aim. This time the results were a bit different. Through the glass I caught the niggah that was sitting in the backseat. He gave out a loud yell as his body jolted back and he dropped his pistol. Once his people noticed, they regrouped back inside the SUV. They continued firing their guns as they sped off down the street. The last I saw of them was a nickel-plated Mossberg being pulled back inside.

I turned to my man, who was on the ground convulsing. The blood running out of his mouth confirmed that he wasn't going to make it. I got on the ground with him and held him in my arms. "CALL A FUCK-ING AMBULANCE!" I shouted to anyone who was listening. "Don't worry, my niggah, I got you; yeah, I got you. Everything's gonna be just fine," I said, rocking him back and forth. When I looked down at him, his face was fearful. He knew there was no coming back from this. He just wanted to make sure he wasn't dying for nothing.

"Yyyyyy-you . . . you tell mmmmy . . . maaaa-ma . . . I lo-lo-love . . . her. Yoooo-you . . . killll them fo—"

Before he could finish his sentence, his mouth stopped moving. Right then, I knew what time it was. My niggah was gone. I couldn't believe it. "Not my niggah, man. Not by a bullet that was meant for me," I said, tears in my eyes. All I could do was grip the handful of his shirt I had clutched so tightly. My people kept pulling and tug-ging on me, telling me to get up. The cops were coming and we had to get out of there. It took me a minute. I was stuck and couldn't move. I couldn't just leave my dude there like he was nothing, like I'd had no part in this shit.

As much as I wanted to stay and face my consequences, my crew wouldn't allow it. Even the onlookers who stood around were telling me to get up out of there. What really broke me apart was looking up and seeing his big sister looking down at me. She extended her arm to grab my hand, assisting me in standing. Before I could properly apologize, she placed her hand over my lips.

"He loved you, baby, and I know you loved him. You get those bastards and you give him the street justice he deserves. That's how you pay me back. This ain't your fault; you need to know that. Now, you get on out of here and call me later to let me know you're safe. Now, go on and get going."

For weeks, I hunted that niggah down. Sleep was not an option. I was like a zombie out there day and night. I walked the Earth high and low, trying to find his ass. There was no sign of him anywhere. I was paying bitches to set him up, but they couldn't even get ahold of the niggah. After about a month of searching, this chick I knew from across the tracks approached me. She confirmed that the niggah had ended up getting killed trying to sneak back into Oakland to visit his mother.

Even though he was no longer with us, the shit still didn't set right with me. Him being dead, cool. Him dying by another niggah's gun, not cool at all. Ain't no way this niggah was supposed to leave the building without being escorted out by me or one of mine.

■ ■ ■

As time went on, I was still doing what needed to be done to get to the top. Ever since I was nine, I'd had the same dream. In the dream, I could see myself living in luxury. I was surrounded by beaucoup money, a big-ass house, and expensive whips. I mean, I could see the shit and I wasn't even living it yet. In my mind, I always told myself I was going to make that dream come true. Those were the last words I said to my father, so it was mandatory. I felt like God must be keeping me here for a reason. I had lost some of my most influential friends, which I rarely talk about because of the memories. I'd had more close calls than I could count. I felt like there must be a destiny for me to fulfill.

As just one example, back when I was seventeen, I hadn't yet gotten with Nita. She and I happened to bump heads in the club, so we copped a seat together and began really getting to know one another. We kicked it off really good. When the time rolled around for the club to close, somehow I ended up getting into a confrontation with these niggaz I knew nothing about. To my mind, we flushed that shit down the drain when we went our separate ways. I thought the situation was over, but apparently not.

A few weeks went by, and the incident was far out of my mind. For a long time, I wasn't knowing these niggaz resided in the same neighborhood as Nita did. When I did find out, it didn't stop me from visiting. I was just smarter about the way I did it . . . or at least I thought I was.

I was creeping out the house one night, about three in the morning. I guess the niggaz caught sight of me; either that or they were already watching and waiting for me. Just as I got in my car, I saw some lights pop on behind me, halfway down the block, like they had been on a stakeout. As I slowly pulled off, so did they. I made a few turns to see if they were really following me, and sure enough, they were.

A couple of my partners had been sleeping in the car, waiting on me. I wasn't going to tell them we were being followed, but before I knew it, I had a face full of glass fragments from a shattered window. I looked at the rearview mirror and saw a gun barrel as long as my arm. I was thinking, *Damn! Is that even a handgun?* There were also shots coming from the other side of the vehicle. I looked at the door frame next to the window and there was a big-ass hole right by my head.

They continued their pursuit, firing shots. I knew that once I got a chance to pull over, my Monte Carlo would be barely recognizable. I had to get these niggaz off my ass so I could protect my homies. Thinking quickly, I turned down a dark alley and killed the lights so they wouldn't be able to see us jumping out that muthafucka. Halfway down the alley, we was about to dive out, until I remembered there was a store a block or two away. It had to be full of people even at this hour. That was our only shot at getting out this alive.

I put the pedal to the metal. It was dark, and my vision was a little blurry from the drink I'd had back at Nita's house. All I could do was pray, asking God to please see me through this night. I had the store in view, but my niggaz were in my ear telling me to speed up.

"Man, shut the fuck up and let me drive this mothafucka!" I shouted, trying to stay focused.

Right when I pulled into the parking lot, I had to do an unexpected swerve to avoid hitting a couple making out by their car. I ended up losing control of the wheel. Fortunately, we were able to dive out of the car before it made impact. As we combat-rolled on the ground, the car smacked dead into a tree, damn near splitting in half. When we got to our feet, we quickly ran for the store's entrance. I looked behind us to make sure they weren't following us into the store, putting other people's lives in danger. As I looked back, I couldn't believe it—they had turned their car around and were still in pursuit.

We headed inside and told everyone to get the fuck down. We even told the clerk to lock the fucking doors. Once inside, we took cover. The only things on my mind were my other dead homies, Backwood and Rome. All I could see was the last looks they'd given me before closing their eyes for the last time, never to open them again. Each time, the last thing I remember was looking up to the sky and telling my partners that I would be joining them one day.

I heard the brakes screeching, then the car came to a complete stop. They didn't immediately exit it. You can't even begin to imagine what was going through our heads as we watched them sit there in their car, just staring into the store. The driver then pulled out his piece and aimed it at the store window. Before he got the chance to fire a shot, the sound of sirens filled the air. Those dudes took off and disappeared into the night. That was our cue to get out of there.

My niggah Curvy saw blood running down my face and thought I was shot. Luckily, I was only cut up from the glass. This was in 2000, right before Valentine's Day.

Despite situations like these, I never felt like I wasn't going to survive, succeed, and make money. My dreams communicated my destiny, plus I know what I'm capable of. I'm a hustler and that's what I do—I'm going to get that money one way or the other.

■ ■ ■

Let me take you on a tour of my incarceration. On November 29 of 2011 I was sentenced to eight years in the joint. While I was in prison, all I did was blow through the money I had. My room looked like a mini supermarket. I had about thirty big bags of chips stashed under my bed and about twenty more tucked off in a few of my partners' rooms. I had about ten cases of sodas scattered throughout the unit. I had about a hundred packs of noodles, a hundred sausages, a hundred packs of bagged beans and rice, and spaghetti. I had all the vegetables and blocks of cheese. I mean, I had it all. I had plenty of canteen. I had so much shit, and that's because I used to send money to other cats' books and give them a list of everything I needed. I also blew a lot of money on gambling; that was a big habit of mine.

Even in the joint, you could feel the envy crawling up under your skin. For certain, broke niggaz didn't like the lifestyles of the big spenders. Every weekend the guard would bring in a TV and we'd have movie night. The microwave area looked like a commercial kitchen, with half the unit scrambling back and forth preparing their special dishes for the night. The shit was crazy.

In prison, I learned the true abilities of a microwave. How niggaz could take a pack of noodles, smash them down into pieces, pour a little oil over them, and fry that shit as a rice substitute. Guys would oil a tortilla, shape it, and fry it crisp in the microwave—then they'd fill it up with toppings.

One of the best inmate dishes was called the rice bowl. To make it, you take a Tupperware bowl and layer the bottom with nacho chips. After that, you add the rice noodles, a layer of black beans, then the cheese. Next, you add the sausages, onions, bell peppers, and tomatoes, sprinkling a final layer of cheese over that. For a big-boy bowl, you would repeat the whole process on top of that. Dudes were making prison pizzas that looked and tasted better than any pizza chain you could think of.

Now, don't get me wrong, I'm not glorifying prison in no sense. I'm not saying that when people go to prison all they do is cook and watch movies. What I'm saying is that some people come out with skills they'd never dreamt of prior to confinement. Maybe incarceration was a debt that needed to be paid to unlock those gifts God had given some in the first place. You know the saying: It's designed that some people will have to learn the hard way. I was one of these people, but prison couldn't really help me with my profession, which was hustling.

In no way did I get my rapping ability from prison, since I was doing that shit way before serving time. What I did get from prison was a clear understanding and sense of who I was and where I was headed in life. One thing prison will do is bring out the real you. It exposes the fake and edifies those pursuing greatness. Prison has produced many realtors, lawyers, authors, business-minded individuals, and so forth. Doing time has its ups and its downs.

One time between bids, I got out with practically nothing. Actually, I didn't have shit—so you know I had to make shit shake. I got back up with my niggah Bleek.

Bleek was my little niggah, or should I say more like my little brother. I can't say in life that I ever had anyone else I was close enough with to address them with that title. This was my dude. Wherever we went, whether it was the park, the club, or the mall, it didn't matter. I made sure he was right there with me and fresh from head to toe. If I got a pack, trust and believe me, he was getting something out of it. If it was a brick, it was guaranteed he was getting a four-and-a-split. It was a must that I kept him straight.

Bleek and I were just connected like that. Whatever the situation was, we went through it together. He was always there by my side. I considered him as my brother and I didn't play about him. Everyone knew there were consequences for fucking with little bro. The little niggah was special too, like he really found a way into my heart. He was loyal and he believed and trusted in me, and I honored him for that. We did everything together. As I was there for him, he was there for me as well. In the end, it was always him and me.

The first time we met, Bleek was like twelve years old. I think I was about fifteen, something like that, and I was already involved in the streets. At that time, I was hustling weed to make ends meet. Pops was on that shit, so Moms and I had to be each other's backbone. Bleek approached me with his partial swag and tried to cop some weed.

"Ah, which one of y'all is Boosie?" After hearing my name, I turned to see who was inquiring. When I saw it was a kid, my first instinct was that he was the little brother of some chick I probably knocked off, coming to deliver a message or some shit. You know, Boosie loves the kids, so I wasn't going to kick him to the curb without hearing him out.

"What it do, little niggah, who you is?" I inquired in a tone that would probably intimidate most shorties his age.

"They call me Bleek, big bro. I heard you got that good gas—I'm trying to put a quarter in the tank, you fucking with it or what?" Like I said, partial swag, but I was kinda impressed. I looked the little niggah up and down and told him to get lost, but not before explaining my reason.

"Ah, little niggah, I'm not about to be added to the count of people who are already partaking in fucking up yo life. No disrespect or hard feelings, but I can't do that one, feel me?" Afterwards, I turned my back on him and continued conversing with my people. The little niggah wasn't trying to hear that, so he grabbed me by the arm and basically demanded I stop and sell him some weed. I have to say, the little niggah was pretty persistent. After a while, I ended up giving in.

We were both from Cross the Tracks and he stayed right across from us on Wyoming Street. From that day on, he was coming to cop weed every day. I didn't know where the little niggah was getting his money from, but he damn sure kept some. I began to take a liking to him after that.

I remember one time we were out on the block and he came through to hang with us. Some lame-ass dude he knew must have spotted him, and he began fucking with him. I guess the niggah was trying to show out since my little homie was surrounded by plenty of girls from the hood. When I looked over, I caught him all in my little niggah's face and pushing him around. Whatever the case might have been, neither my crew nor I liked the shit. My man had seen the shit and pointed it out to me. We went up to the dude and put him in his place, letting him know that an incident like that was never to be seen nor heard about ever again. After that, we canned the niggah off the block: my man sent him off with a swift kick up the ass.

I took Bleek under my wing and he became a part of my every-day existence. Come to find out, we had so much shit in common. His family was full of goons and killers, just like mine—not to mention dope dealers and crackheads as well. I realized he actually didn't need our help that time when he was being picked on. All he had to do was make one call and I'm pretty sure that dude would've been lying under somebody's porch. It was actually a blessing on dude's behalf that we'd come to Bleek's aid instead of his family doing it.

He took to me because every time he saw me I was on the grind. I was still trying to get back everything I'd lost while I was in prison. The block was booming, and business was picking up more and more every day. Eventually, my clientele began knocking on my grandmother's door asking for product, so I had to move my action. I relocated to Wyoming Street, right by Bleek's crib, and that's when we really began jamming together. From that point on, he never left my side, and things seemed to be getting better. Times were good; I mean, we had some sweet days together. We were at it, neck and neck, like twins. We were shopping, fucking bitches, and burning up the block.

Everything was great . . . until the day Bleek died. That's when my world changed for the worst. He was gunned down in 2010. It was fucked up because the shit happened the year I was being indicted on first-degree murder charges and already serving a sentence of ten years on multiple drug possession charges. When I found out, the shit really hurt my heart. I think I cried for like two weeks behind that incident.

Although I was tucked away for a minute, my little niggah was still in the streets making shit happen. He was using the game I'd taught him and making it work for himself. Word was, my little brother was trying to cop some weight from this niggah. Apparently, the niggah he was copping from had a price on his head: some niggaz were on his heels because he was supposed to be taking the stand on one of their partners.

Word got back to me that while Bleek was sitting in the car checking out the product, another car pulled up alongside them with the windows already down. Before they could even react, multiple shots ripped through the car. It was said the killers didn't even bother to flee the scene right away. Supposedly they stuck around to make sure the hit was completed. Once the kill was confirmed, they sped off on screeching tires. My little niggah was just caught in the wrong place at the wrong time.

I couldn't believe it. Those niggaz didn't have to kill my little brother. I know they saw him. I know they saw him! I know they saw Bleek. He didn't have shit to do with them. All they had to do was pull back. They could've caught the other niggah some other time. Now my little niggah is gone. Again I had lost everything while in prison—because that's what he was to me, everything.

I also found out that my cousin Donkey was in the car during the time it happened. That's my older cousin next to Trell. I guess they didn't see him in the backseat when they opened fire. When I talked to him, he said everything happened so fast. He said it fucked him up mentally once he got out the back of the car and was able to look in Bleek's eyes, being that he died with them open.

I'm glad Donkey survived though, because he and I are close. Donkey stands about five-eight and at the time weighed around one eighty to two hundred pounds. He always had that intense Sean Penn look on his face. The niggah was a straight maniac. The man acted as if he didn't care about anything or anyone. He and I even got into it a few times.

One time, I was trying to cop some work from one of my plugs and Donkey was with me. The deal went down smooth, but I got a call later that night from my plug. He explained to me that I had only two options: to bring him his money back or bring my gun with me next time. I didn't know what the fuck he was talking about. Then he went on telling how I was out of order for bringing a niggah through there to rob him. Right then, I knew who he was referring to. I tried telling him I had nothing to do with it, but I would holla at Donkey and try to get his money back. Once we disconnected, I dialed Donkey's number. As soon as he picked up the phone, I went in on him. He wasn't trying to hear the shit though. I told him he needed to make things right and give the money back. He told me I was out of my mind. He then said if anybody tried to come retrieve the cash, he would be putting them in a body bag. Like I said, the man was crazy. He used to go around terrorizing people for no reason at all.

One day, his luck almost ran out. Word was he was at the store copping some blunts, and the plug who he had robbed ended up stopping at the same gas station. The thing is, he wasn't alone. When he caught sight of Donkey, he quickly remembered his face. He rounded up his boys and filled them in on what had happened. They weren't too happy about it. They headed back out and waited for Donkey outside.

Whomever he was on the phone with had his attention because he didn't even see the four niggaz standing there with guns in their hands. Before he had the chance to react, bullets rained down on him, splattering the store's front entrance. Donkey's body was pushed back from the impact of so many rounds, knocking him backwards, causing him to crash through the store window. As he lay there covered in shattered glass, the plug walked up and stood over him. Looking down on him, he asked if he knew who he was. When Donkey replied no, the plug told him not to worry, God would explain it to him. He then fired one round into D's face before walking off.

The crazy shit about it is that the niggah actually survived. I was thinking, *Damn! What the fuck is this niggah?* He spent about sixteen months in the hospital before making a full recovery, but once he did, the hunt was on. He searched the streets, trying to find the whereabouts of the plug. One day, he got a tip from an anonymous caller, a female. The little birdie told him that if he was still looking for the plug, he could be found laid up at some bitch's house. She then gave him the address and he was on his way.

Once he located the spot, he parked his car around the corner and walked back to the house. He first walked around to see what the block was looking like. He wanted to make sure shit was clear; he wasn't really in the mood for extra body count. There was a small entrance leading under the porch. He crawled under there and camped out until his prey exited the house.

After a few hours had gone by, he finally heard the door open and a bit of conversation. He removed an all-black forty-five with the lemon squeeze from his hoodie pocket. Quietly, he eased out from under the porch. He didn't even bother to dust himself off. He waited until he heard the front door close and footsteps coming down the stairs. He came from around the side of the house and got the plug's attention. He tiptoed behind him and yelled, "Hey, niggah!"

As soon as the plug turned around, he was greeted by the butt of the gun. He stumbled backwards until he was lying on his side holding his face, trying to stop the blood that was spilling out the wound. His eyes widened with disbelief when he looked at Donkey's face. All he kept repeating was "I killed you, dog. Naw, you dead, niggah! I killed you, dog!" Donkey stood over him and asked the plug if he remembered him. Then he continued, "You were right—God explained it to me." Then he returned the favor of shooting the plug in the face. He shot him a second time, making sure there was no round-trip ticket.

Now you see what I mean when I tell you the niggah was missing more than a few screws? He has been through a number of things, I have to admit. The niggah was shot in the face twice, once when he was twelve and again when he was older. Plus, he accidentally shot my cousin in the face. He was even in an incident that left his car hanging off the bridge over the Mississippi River. So, yeah, he's been through it.

Chapter 11

PRISON AND LIFE ON DEATH ROW

Me and Tootie at the Dixon Correctional Institute in 2010.

L ife on the streets was crazy. I was into all types of shit. Whatever it took to keep my mind off certain things was what I was
into. Niggaz were hating, bitches were messy, and I was front-
ing the police every month. You have to watch the police because
them bitches are greedy as hell. They have no respect for a Black
man in the South. They used to always be in my shit, tearing my car
apart, looking for illegal substances.

It got to the point where they were pulling me over every chance
they got. They'd snatch me out the car and deprive me of all the cash
that was in my pockets. I would just look at them and be like, "How the
fuck y'all gonna just take my money? I ain't even do shit. Man, fuck y'all
dirty-ass, crooked-ass cops. Y'all need to let me go." I knew I hadn't
done shit wrong and I damn sure didn't have nothing incriminating

on me. I was smarter than that. I knew how they were, so if I did have a pack on me, there was no way I was pulling over.

Those muthafuckas worse than the criminals. Little did they know, I placed my phone on record the moment they got on my ass. If they were on some bullshit, we were going to find out about it that day, you feel me?

Now, I can remember one night I was riding, minding my business and handling a situation that needed to be handled. I had a four-and-a-split of cocaine on me and one of those bitches ended up getting right behind me. I was just pulling up to the stoplight when he flashed his red-and-blues on me. I was looking in my rearview like, *This muthafucka ain't got shit better to do?* I wasn't about to lose what I had and I sure wasn't about to go back to prison. He pulled from behind me and pulled along my right side. He then signaled for me to roll my window down. I shook my head, like "hell naw." I had a burning blunt in my hand and the car smelt like hella weed. He looked like he was trying to radio for backup, so I hit that left on him real quick. Once I made that turn, I checked my rearview to see what his next move would be. Of course he pursued me. Soon as he swerved around the oncoming traffic, I opened the engine up on that bitch. I was burning the road.

I had to think quickly and I mean fast as hell. The way I took off on that punk at the stoplight, I knew he'd have animosity with me. Ain't no telling what his intentions would be if he got ahold of me. I'm sweating, heart beating and hands shaking. If I hadn't been a fan of

Martin Luther King before that night, it sure as hell made me one—all I kept hearing were those freedom bells ringing. The last thing I needed was for that day to end with me making a collect call to my kids.

I was speeding through the city streets, doing about a hundred miles an hour. I had to put some distance between us before he had the chance to put his beams on my plates. Did I mention I had this girl in the passenger seat, screaming all in my fucking ear? She was telling me to pull over and let her out. That had to have been one of the dumbest women I have ever dealt with.

I ended up making it as far as the graveyard before I opened the door and was about to bail out, but the bitch kept grabbing me by the arm, trying to stop me.

"Hell naw, niggah! What the fuck you think you doing? You're not about to jump out this bitch and leave me in here with this motha-fucka still rolling! Naw, fuck that shit!" I looked at her like she was crazy or something. I snatched my arm away from her then pushed her off me.

"What the fuck is wrong with you, are you going to stash the shit for me?"

Immediately she said, "Hell naw!" With that, my decision was made. I left that muthafucka in gear so the cop would have to go after the car instead of me. I didn't want the bitch to get hurt, even though she'd left me hanging. I brought the speed down to around ten miles per hour so I could pull off my stunt. As soon as I made my exit, I heard the sound of my open door slamming into a tombstone. I knew that was fucked up, but I had bigger things to worry about.

Once I rolled out that mothafucka, I quickly made it back to my feet. I then headed for the shadows to stay as invisible as possible. When I had enough of a lead, I tossed the dope in a secure spot and ran like it was dogs chasing me. It was only a Monte Carlo, so I didn't care about the damage or even getting it back.

The car wasn't registered to me, so if they ran the plates they would never link it back to me. I made sure to take all my illegal substances with me so the crazy broad I was with couldn't get in trouble. Since at that time she had only known me by my street nickname, there wasn't much she could say.

At the end of the day, victory was mine. I managed to get away from those bitches. I even went back to recover the dope I had tossed. Now, that's a clean getaway. I was pissed though. I had been an idiot. What the fuck was I thinking? I knew better than to have any amount of shit on me, let alone that amount. That wasn't my MO. I didn't usually rock like that, and I don't know what had possessed me to do it at that moment.

■ ■ ■

Going back, I was into a lot of shit during my juvenile years. I was rounding up plenty of cases back then, not knowing it would affect my future if I didn't change for the better. I think my first charge was for some petty stealing, nothing really serious.

Let me detail another incident that took place during my adolescent years. At thirteen, my boy Curt and I used to run into Dillard's and stack all the Polo shirts in a pile, then tear up outta there with them. I knew they were valued at top dollar, so I used to take them to the hood and off them to all the dealers for thirty or forty bucks apiece. The shit became a ritual. After a while, they started getting suspicious. It was only a matter of time before they were chasing me and my partner up out of there. Them bitches got on my ass one day. I hauled up out of there and they chased me all the way to Fun Fair Park. Yeah, I was feeling a bit sluggish that day, so they ended up getting lucky.

I was young and dumb, so I was going on what I called "an experience spree" for the next few years. Then, on my seventeenth birthday, I was out on some stupid shit, which resulted in me going to jail. It was me, Chug, and one of my other little partners. We were on the streets wilding out, hanging out the car window, blowing weed smoke in the air like we were unstoppable. I had some zips of coke on me, Chug had a thirty clip hanging out his jeans, and my little partner had a rod on him as well. Out of nowhere, the cops got behind us and immediately turned on their flashers. Without delay, we jumped out that bitch and hauled ass. See, in them days we had a system. We put vehicles in certain names where we could retrieve them if towed, but the police couldn't trace them back directly to us.

I came to a house that had an opening to the porch and slid up under it, not knowing I'd stay there for the remainder of the night. While I was under there just chilling, I could hear footsteps approaching. To my surprise, I saw my partner run past. This muthafucka then ran under the same porch I was under.

Before I had a chance to say anything, I saw the police dogs scouting the area. Apparently, they were chasing him. They went past the part of the porch where he was hiding and came straight to my area and wasted no time sinking their teeth into me, damn near killing me. I literally had to play dead in order for them to stop gnawing on me. Of course I was arrested, and I ended up going to the hospital to get stitches in my head and lip. Right after, I was transferred to Parish Prison, so my seventeenth birthday was spent in confinement. For the next three or four days, I was on the inside looking out.

A couple of months down the line, I was arrested again. I was released and arrested again months later on a six-month remand. My life became a cycle of going in and out of jail. Plus a year prior my CEO, C-Loc, had gone to prison on a five-year bid, so I didn't feel much hope.

■ ■ ■

People would always ask me, how did I handle being locked up? I had to explain to them that my life is not just words on paper or a role in a movie. This thug shit is in my blood for real. I don't do this for likes, revenue, or attention; I'm really a street niggah. When I first got arrested on murder charges, they were talking about locking me in the hole in protective custody. Fuck that! I said I wasn't going. I demanded that I be placed inside general population with the other inmates.

The warden was trying to keep me locked in a little-ass cell until I was either acquitted or released. The shit was ridiculous. Whether you're in prison or not, you still have human rights. I guess they thought I feared going into the population of about three hundred inmates, but it didn't bother me at all. I wanted to go into the population because you can live much better. I couldn't see myself wasting away in a cell with no one to associate with. Besides, I wasn't ducking any drama. I had made a name for myself, so I didn't believe anyone would allow any harm to come to me. I believed everyone would get a fair shake.

I was raised by my uncles, who had always informed me that if you aren't up on your shit, it will be easy for you to get popped. They also said if you stayed in your cell, you would be safe. That's just how it was. You were safer in your cell if you weren't built for it. One's main focus should be to get home in one piece. Population is risky for those unaware of its dangers. There were too many niggaz to keep an eye on. There were at least three hundred niggaz around you at night. Prison is also a place for one to make moves if need be. For instance, a niggah could easily make thirty to forty thousand dollars a month in jail, especially if you had rank—then you were more likely controlling the tickets.

Prison life is similar to the streets but operates a little differently. For instance, postage stamps are considered as real cash. To buy anything, you need stamps. Life in prison doesn't move without them. Commissary, food, sport, hygiene, etc., is all on account of stamps.

You'd be surprised at the people who confine themselves to a cell. I didn't blame other rappers for staying in their cells. Even if the guards chose to keep you in a cell, you could have your lawyer call up there to get you placed amongst the other inmates, especially if you aren't in population confinement. It's your given right.

In prison, you're either a gangster or prey. I was cut like that, so I had no worries. Jail ain't nothing but another form of the hood. With all the valid niggaz to bump heads with and activities going on, who would want to be alone in a cell? Of course, jail is a fucked-up place to be. But if you have to be there, it's more live when you're in the population.

The shit be jumping off for real. Like, niggaz be up all night gambling, fucking off on the phone with different bitches, not to mention the contact visits. The shit was live. Being alone in a cell will eventually drive you crazy. Stuck in a fucking box with all that shit on your mind is unhealthy. Now, if you're a rat, then that's a different matter. That's more than reason enough to separate yourself from others.

When you first hit the population, niggaz will have some of the older guys come to you to motivate you. If you're walking with your head down, one of the old heads will come check up on you. Niggaz are in there with life sentences; no one wants to hear a short-timer complaining. Newcomers are always yapping about what they've lost by being there.

During my sixty-day stay, I was conflict-free. Of course there were a couple of niggaz running around there, fat-mouthing through the bars, but you know how people get down. Everyone wants to have something to say, especially about a celebrity.

■ ■ ■

I remember being locked up and finding out they had arrested my baby's mother on a visit. The charges were for bringing drugs into the system. She had marijuana, cocaine, syrup, and synthetic. They were indicting me for the shit. This was around the same time I was indicted for the murders. It pissed me off for them to involve her in my mess, but I knew she'd stand strong.

They began questioning her about my alleged crimes. She kept telling them she wasn't talking and that she was going to remain quiet until she spoke with a lawyer. I believed in her because we had history together. Once I got the discovery back, I knew where her loyalties lay. I had all the paperwork, so everything she'd said was in black and white. Immediately, I reached out to her. When she picked up, she began crying and saying how sorry she was. She explained that facing off with detectives was much worse than arguing with cops on the streets. I wasn't trying to hear that shit. She'd sold me out. I just said fuck it and took the lick like the man I am.

Had it been another chick, then I'd probably believe she was out for blood. Once I got the chance to chop it up with her and actually look into her eyes, I knew that everything she said was authentic. I could see the love she had for me, but at the same time, her fear was more visible than ever. The fear of going to prison, of not being able to raise her child—it was a bit more than she could handle. The way her body trembled kind of fucked me up. She didn't deserve that shit and I had no right putting her in that position. At the same time, when you say ride or die, that's the way the shit is supposed to be.

That was in 2010. The fight was on, and I rounded up some of the best lawyers I could afford. Now it was time to blow my money on something more productive, which was my freedom. That's what the shit came down to. I remained trill to the fullest. I knew they didn't have shit on me. I was just hoping the media wouldn't convict me.

My case was heavily publicized. My face was on the TV screen every day. Shortly after the charges, I began court. Have you ever seen the movie *S.W.A.T.*? That's how I was led into court: eight cars in back of me, eight in the front, and two on each side. They wanted me to look guilty before I was even on trial.

The media was promoting my conviction better than my label ever promoted my music. I'm not saying my label did a bad job— I'm saying the media went extra hard with it. During that time, I was going through a lot. It was so much that I actually had to start leaning on something or someone bigger than myself, and the only person I could think of was God.

I became a prayer warrior. I could be anywhere and just start praying. I finally understood why my mother used to tell me that I needed to pray. Through most of my trials and tribulations she'd be like, "Boy, what you need to do is pray. Get down on those knees of yours and ask Him for forgiveness, baby, but first you have to accept Him as your Lord and Savior." Believe it or not, the shit actually worked. There had been many situations where, if it had not been for God's grace, I'd probably be stretched out in some morgue. I also had to lean toward my family and friends. At the same time, I couldn't show any weakness no matter what I was going through. I had to remain sane, so I was clowning every day. I was doing all types of shit, anything to keep my mind off my troubles.

This is prison we're talking about, so the ways I could release my stress was to smoke, drink, and work out, not to mention spending time on the phone with women. Niggaz used to try to talk to me about my case, but I would always tell them to shut the fuck up and leave me the fuck alone. I was on death row. Who wants to be in that position? The shit would piss me off, the remarks those niggaz would make—shit like "Boosie, you on TV again." I'm right next to the niggah! I'm looking at him like, *You see me sitting here? You don't think I see myself?* I knew some of the inmates meant well because they would always be reaching out to me. But in a place like that, you can't win—instead the muthafuckas always win. Once the white man's got you, he's sure to keep his foot on your neck.

I had to stay busy, so I began to increase my rap sheet. I don't mean my criminal record, I'm speaking more on my rap tablets. Yeah, I was writing my ass off. With so much going on, it gave me so much to write about. With so much bad publicity, you gotta think about the shit they hear and the picture they paint of you. They were definitely trying to bury me. That was what made writing so important to me: It was my way of venting. It was my escape route. When I was angry, I'd pick up a pen. When I was feeling good or something good happened, I'd pick up a pen. Music gave me complete freedom. I was able to release everything in me that felt toxic.

Once I made it home, all I had to do was get with the producer and make the sound. We'd freak it a bit and make a hit record.

Chapter 12

SURVIVING THE ODDS

Me with my mom and C-Murder—
free C-Murder for real.

I remember one time I was arrested and sent to prison. It all started over a bogus-ass traffic stop. I was riding one night, just minding my business, when suddenly my car's interior was lit up with disco lights. The cops had gotten on my ass and turned on their flashers. I pulled over to the side of the road to find out what the problem was. Although I knew I hadn't done anything wrong, I did have a gun and a little bit of weed on me. My gun was legal and in my name, so I didn't feel it would be a problem. I threw the weed under the car, but they eventually found it.

I did have some prior weed charges on me. Also, I had three assault charges and a battery charge for pistol-whipping a niggah. That started because this niggah named Sneeze played me. I had copped some work from the niggah just to see what he was working with. The shit looked, smelled, and cooked good as hell. The only thing is that, when it came time for the tester, the shit didn't pan out like it was supposed to. That shit had me heated. When I got back up with the niggah, he called himself tongue wrestling and spit boxing. I just couldn't understand the shit, and after hearing this cat rambling on and on like he couldn't be touched, I had to dead-end that shit.

There were a lot of people out that night. I guess that gave him a boost of confidence. The niggah had the audacity to point his finger in my face. I didn't even have time to think—immediately I went into beast mode. I removed a pistol from my waistline and ejected the clip. I took a swing and smacked him across the face with the gun. He stumbled back a few steps like he was moonwalking, then he fell to the ground. I walked up on the niggah and started smacking him repeatedly, exercising my moral right to fuck him up. And that was that. Of course the cops were called, but I was able to get away.

Ever since that night, they had been looking for me, so I'd expected this. I was cuffed and taken to jail. I received a couple of years for the gun and for pistol-whipping the guy; the other charges were dropped.

I was being held at Hunt Correctional Center. It's located in the Black neighborhood down by Baton Rouge. After a few days there, I was shipped up north to Winnfield. I resided there for about two months. Then I was transferred to DCI. I stayed there for about eight months. When I caught my indictment for the murder charges, I was shipped to death row at Angola—because when you're fighting a murder charge in Louisiana, you could go to death row without being convicted. I knew it was a bunch of bullshit, being they'd pressured someone to lie on me.

Once I found out I was being indicted and placed on death row at Angola, I called my lawyer and asked him what the fuck was going on. "Why the fuck am I being sent to Angola?" He explained the reason they gave was that I had been involved in some sort of inmate shit, which they'd made up on me. I didn't know what they were talking about, and I sure as hell didn't want to be in there. The authorities felt that Angola was the only prison where I wouldn't be able to manipulate the other inmates.

I was immediately sent to the population. I had a lot of anger in me because I felt derailed. I was thinking, *How the hell did I get sent to the joint without even being offered rehab first?* I'm a fuckin' weedhead, so that should've been my first option. I couldn't believe they'd hit me with all those charges. Every charge was under seven grams, which only called for rehab.

They had this one guy in there who'd pulled this thing with AA. He had nine convictions for crack and possession of heroin, and that niggah ended up getting rehab. The inconsistency was really pissing me off. I knew I had caught the gun case, but it was a legal heater. What the fuck? I'm a legal human being and my gun was legal. Even with that, they hit a niggah with two to eight years and suspended my permit. I stood up like, "Come on, man. Y'all can't be serious?" I looked at my lawyer, who just stood there looking dumbfounded. So yeah, I was pissed.

While I was locked up, I happened to bump into C-Murder, who was also fighting a murder charge. He was one of those guys who did his time without it hindering him in any way. He was there long before I was. After seeing the way I was moving, he tried to preach to me. I guess my showing a lack of discipline upset him. He used to tell me I was too wild and sooner or later, I'd realize I couldn't beat the system. I understood how he felt, but I wasn't trying to hear any of that. I used to tell him I was going to win at this thing—I hadn't come to prison to be a good guy. I'm a thug and that shit don't stop at the gate. We're criminals, man, so what do you expect?

I was younger than he was, so for us to be facing the same charges weighed a little heavier on me. With all the shit I was going through, I had to smoke weed. It was the only thing that kept me sane. Even acknowledging that, he'd still tell me, "Man, you're going to lose this thing if you don't get it together." He might have been right, but at the time, I was in my rebellious mode. To me, it felt good beating the system sometimes.

C was more mature than I was, so he looked at things a little differently. He basically spent his time reading books and working on his case. I had much respect for him. He was like a big brother to me while I was up in that place. We even slept in the same cell. I was on the top bunk and he took the bottom bunk. At night, he'd sit me down and try talking some sense into me. I loved the attention and the fact that he cared, but at the same time I also liked messing around and having fun in jail. I liked playing practical jokes on the other inmates, throwing water on people, and setting booby traps in their rooms. In prison, you have to make the best out of the worst situations, and that's what I did. Nobody was going to see me walking around with a sad face.

There was this one older guy who had been locked up with us on death row. He used to tell me, "Say, young'un, you have to be one of the dumbest criminals I've ever met in my life. You walk around this bitch all day playing, starting shit with the guards, and acting as if life and everything in it submits to you. What you need to do is start taking your situation a little more seriously because niggaz is watching."

Now, I could have done the logical thing and said fuck you or gone upside the niggah's head for being all in my business, but I felt his pain. I knew where he was coming from. He was feeling like C— knowing what a lifer would give for any opportunity at freedom. In their eyes, I was throwing away my chances for freedom. There was some truth to what he said, but I was like, "Man, what the fuck you expect me to do? You prefer I just sit around and cry all day? Hell naw! I'm going to live it up to the fullest."

■ ■ ■

My hardest times in prison weren't from seeing my kids on visitation. It was watching them from behind as they made their departure. They were my strength. My whole purpose for going so hard was all for them. They gave me the motivation I needed to achieve my goals.

Other than missing them, prison was a walk in the park. I would be clowning. I had to keep a light mood, being how some of the other guys were so depressed and down. I used to try to lift their spirits and let them know there was still hope. A lot of those guys had low self-esteem. A few of them even went as far as to hang themselves. I felt like: *Damn, if I had talked to them or made them laugh, then maybe they wouldn't have done the shit.*

C thought I was weird for the way I thought at times, but he was my boy. Free C-Murder for real. I will always look to him as a brother, being we did four and a half years together. I shouldn't have been in there in the first place, but I did have those assault charges. Like I said, I went in there mad as hell. Since those muthafuckas wanted to send me up, I knew what I was going to do in there. I was already locked up, so I figured I might as well continue being a criminal. I mean, what the fuck else were they going to do to me?

When I first walked through those prison gates, I was feeling like *fuck everything.* All I could think of was how I was going to accumulate funds, because I intended to multiply my shit during my stay. I wasn't the type to go to jail and start reading books or the other shit niggaz do to stay out of trouble. I had to get active—not just for me, but for the financial welfare of my family.

Shortly after my arrival, I settled in and began putting my plays in motion. I was making shit happen. Just like in the streets, I was doing my thing. I was getting the coke at least a quarter key at a time. I had the young niggaz going crazy off the Purple Haze and OG Kush. The white boys loved the coke, but the percs were a perfect replacement when the shit wasn't available. I even had gallons of syrup on deck. Niggaz were going to the hole on the regular because the lean had them bumping into guards and all types of shit. I used to keep that shit by my bedside. Being that they sold two-liters in the canteen, I used those containers to stash my drinks. Everybody had two-liters in their rooms, so they never caught on.

Life was good. I stayed fucked up off the weed or the lean—hell, sometimes both. I probably did more drugs in prison than I did on the streets and that's some crazy shit. I wouldn't fuck with your intelligence—I was really a king in that bitch. You ain't gotta take my word for it; check my rap sheet. A niggah doing time ain't going to lie for a free niggah.

Before getting sentenced, I used to be at the studio, dropping tracks on a regular. When they did sentence me, it was about six months out. Within that six-month time frame, I was lacing the studios with my sound. Then, when I ended up going to jail, I had my people leak the shit. I was locked up, but I had all kinds of music coming out. Three months into my bid, I called the house and told my people to leak another one. My shit was playing everywhere. Niggaz in the joint were lost and couldn't understand how new shit was being released when I was right there with them every day.

■ ■ ■

I spent about three and a half years of my bid at Angola. My eyes stayed widened to my surroundings. There was so much shit going on that I had to stay on point. Like, some shit I had never seen before in my life. One dude who was controlling his cell got down on the floor and told this other niggah, "Ah, niggah, bend over and pick up my bun." I didn't know what the shit meant, but it didn't sound good to me. The shit was crazy. I had to get out of that place. I needed my feet back on solid ground.

I remember sitting at the domino table one day when a few new inmates were brought in. One of them was crying uncontrollably. This one niggah named Shaky saw that shit and decided to capitalize off the situation. Apparently, Shaky had had some confrontations with the niggah's brother while they were on the streets. Whatever the case may be, Shaky used the opportunity to get back at the niggah.

The new guy was escorted to his sleeping quarters to settle in for what appeared to be a life sentence. When lunchtime rolled around, Shaky chose a seat that was close to the tray line. When the new guy grabbed his tray, he stood in the middle of the room looking to see where he would sit. From out of nowhere, Shaky planted his tray in the guy's face. He practically beat that boy half to death. The shit was crazy, yo. That shit opened up my eyes for real.

I got on the phone and called my lawyer. I told him to challenge the indictment. Those muthafuckas didn't have enough to indict me.

I was more driven now than ever before to get that rope from around my neck. When I started coming to my senses, I finally realized the truth behind C-Murder's words and why he read so much. In no time, I was following the same path. I began reading and reading and reading.

You know, I don't always feel this way, but truth be told, I really regret going to prison. I put my people through a lot; it was a hard time for us. On the other hand, a lot of people believe that had I not gone to prison, I probably would have been dead out there on those streets. One thing I know is that God looks out for babies and fools. Sometimes He'll put us in a situation just to get us out of one. At the speed I was going, brakes wouldn't have stopped me before I hit a brick wall. Doing time made me realize the importance of my kids. I wouldn't want to put them or my people through that ever again in their lives.

When I was going from jail to jail, I was making power moves. Being active was the only way to settle my anger. Had I not done that, I probably wouldn't have gotten all that time. Again, it was the hate. When you have so much hate in you, your mind isn't clear. You end up making bad decisions, and I made a lot of them.

I had to be done with that shit. All I kept doing was violating. I kept getting drugs in the joint, clowning around, and doing dumb shit. I didn't really have to do the shit. I knew I should have stopped, but I didn't. I was too addicted to the money. Plus, I still wanted to give my kids, my girl, and my family a good life. Now I feel that was a bad decision. Me making moves ruined a lot of shit, including the relationship with the woman I was in love with.

■ ■ ■

I had accumulated six to seven hundred thousand dollars before going to prison. I ended up spending at least three hundred thousand on lawyer fees, then another three hundred thousand. After that, I had to make another two hundred eighty thousand. Whatever I had left, I ended up blowing over the next three years. I came home with nothing. My mother did have forty thousand put up for me. If it wasn't for Momma, that shit would've been gone. My momma put it up and left it there for three years. It totally shocked me when she presented it to me. I didn't even know she had that left. I thought all the money was gone. My momma was just paying bills and keeping shit afloat, you feel me? I was broke, but it prepared me for that moment. I knew what I had to do.

When they told me I was going to get the death penalty, I was going through it. I knew they were all a bunch of bullshit cases, but I still had thoughts going through my mind: *I wonder if they'll convict me because of who I am and how they're portraying me on the news every day.* All you can do is take it day by day and pray about it, and see what they are going to do. To be honest, there ain't much you can do in a situation like that. If you're a person with strong faith, you'll sit and wait on God to give you the answers. The main thing is not to lose focus and to stay ahead of your situation. Once you start falling short, it's easy to get lost in a realm that completely shuts you out from the world. This will feed your anger and you will continue to spiral.

Altogether, I spent nearly a million on lawyer fees trying to beat the case. I must say, it was one of the best uses for money I have ever spent in my life. Knowing what I was going up against, I had to come with the thunder because the courts were trying to strike me down. I rounded up some of the best defense attorneys money could buy. I had Jason Williams, Martin Ray, and Johnnie Cochran. He was the one who handled the O. J. Simpson trial. If only you could have seen Mr. Cochran in the flesh, the way he trampled over the prosecutors. I was truly impressed, but I give God all the credit. My lawyers did good, but I know it was God making them work.

I probably would've gotten convicted if I were a regular person who had to use a public defender. The reason being, the public defender works for the state. The main purpose of a public defender is to benefit the system. Just because they appoint you a lawyer doesn't mean he's on your side—the state signs his check. So, if your people are ever in a situation, get them a paid lawyer. The state will appoint a lawyer for you who sits down and eats with the prosecution and judge every day.

My case was presented to be more than it was. While I was going to trial, they had snipers on the roof like I was some sort of terrorist or something. They even went as far as having me transported in bulletproof trucks. Hell, they even had police mounted on horses surrounding the truck. According to them muthafuckas, I was having the district attorney followed. They seriously made it look like I was trying to do something to him. Were they serious? I'm a hood niggah; I wasn't making moves like that. Of course they flashed that across the news to put the icing on the cake. They had the man being escorted back and forth to work every day. Even the feds were there babysitting. They made it clear they were about business. One of them said to me, "I don't know, you might beat this murder, but if you come after that public official, you'd better believe we're going to rain hell down on you." They tried everything they could to make me look guilty in the eyes of the world—but mainly in the eyes of the jurors, the ones who held my life in their hands.

They were using everything against me—my music, videos, movies, and all that shit. My lawyer stood up and asked, "Why are you doing this? Clearly this is hatred. Johnny Cash even sang in 'Folsom Prison' that he'd shot a man just to watch him die. It's called creative lyrics, that doesn't mean it's true." But they weren't trying to hear any of that.

Do you know we spent an entire day in court just listening to my music? A whole fuckin' day just to analyze my shit. How the fuck were they going to interpret a rap song that has so much slang in it and they don't even listen to that genre? They couldn't even quote my shit properly. They twisted my words to say what they wanted them to say.

Those bastards even made my mother a witness against me. She had nothing to do with nothing, but they still made her a witness, and that meant she couldn't be in the courtroom with me. She had to stay outside and wait on the courthouse steps. Crazy, right?

On the last day of the trial, they came to my lawyer and asked him if I would take ten to twelve years. "Hell naw," I said, not believing he'd even ask me that shit. I made sure he understood me when I said I wasn't taking nothing! Those muthafuckas knew they were beat. My lawyer knew the shit too. The only reason he'd presented the deal to me was because, as my lawyer, he had to let me know what they were offering.

The case was just bogus in every aspect. When I think about it, I don't believe any jury in the whole country would have convicted me. To make a long story short, not guilty was the verdict. I was acquitted in less than thirty-eight minutes. I was happy when I heard that not-guilty verdict, I ain't gonna lie. I just put my hands up, like, *I'm going home.*

I was sent back to Angola. Dudes were welcoming me with open arms. Niggaz were throwing parties on every line, I mean, making a helluva noise. I had an awesome welcome back.

Once I beat my trial, I was let off death row and sent back to the dorm. Even after that, the guards were coming at me like, "You have to stay in your cell under protective custody."

I was like, "Hell naw. I'm going back to the population so I can see the sun and mingle with the rest of the inmates."

All I kept thinking was, *I'm going home, and I'll get to spend time with my family.* All I wanted was to be back with my family. Beating the case allowed me to have contact visits. Now I was able to touch my kids, kiss them, and feel the beat of their hearts next to mine. No more looking at them through glass. Now I could hug my momma and feel her embrace. I felt as though a miracle had transpired, because God could have killed me so many times. There were times I could have gotten out the car and something drastic could have happened to me. Looking at the situation, I know it was a miracle. Because when I look at old pictures, all my partners are dead.

Chapter 13

A BLESSING
OR A CURSE

When I was born, I wasn't diagnosed with type 1 diabetes, also known as juvenile diabetes. The shit didn't run in my family, so I didn't know how the hell I'd ended up with it. I often asked myself, "Was it the drugs that led me to this point? The endless cups of lean or rotation of blunts? Or maybe it was the Man upstairs giving it to me to make me strong—a way of opening my eyes to understand the power of His right hand."

One of my partners, Head Busser, told me at one point that it was a blessing and a curse. I can understand where he was coming from, because no sooner than I became successful, this heavy burden was laid upon me. Was I given this sickness because of my past wrongdoings? I wondered that at times. When 2003 hit, I felt as if God was punishing me.

For example, one time I was scheduled to do a concert and I ended up puking everywhere right before I was about to take the stage. I didn't allow it to hinder me; I continued with the performance. But when I exited the stage, everything went black. The next time I opened my eyes, I was lying in a hospital bed. When I awakened, my partner Ivy and my momma were at my bedside. The looks on their faces immediately told me something was wrong. Momma had compassion and would dress the truth in a lie if it meant keeping me from going on a mind trip. I knew Ivy would keep it one hundred with me, so I asked him what happened. He looked at me for a second, then looked toward the floor before replying, "Once you were done with your performance, while exiting the stage, you just fainted. There was no time to fuck around, so we got you up and rushed you to the hospital."

Before I had a chance to respond, the doctor entered the room. He approached my bed and told me I had type 1 diabetes. At that moment, I felt like the world was closing in on me. That is a moment I will never forget. The only thing that came out of my mouth was "What the fuck?!"

He looked at me steadily and confirmed, "I'm sorry you had to find out this way, son, but there are ways of treating it." He removed a syringe from the pocket of his long white doctor's coat and began showing me how to inject myself with insulin. He also handed me a booklet indicating the kinds of foods I should and shouldn't be eating. Of course it put me in a slump finding out that all the great dishes that had caught my attention were hazards.

My heart became numb and my eyes were brimming with tears. That was the beginning of a long nightmare. No matter how positive I tried being, I just couldn't bring myself to believe it. How in the hell could that have happened to me all of a sudden? *Maybe I'm dreaming*, I often told myself. *Was it the drugs that led me to this point?*

When the time finally arrived for me to make my departure, I was pissed off and mad at the world. I did not want to believe that I needed insulin in order to be all right. When I was first diagnosed with the shit, I was rarely taking my insulin and I stayed sick most of the time because of it. I couldn't hold my urine for nothing in the world. Often, I would be jumping out of cars, pissing everywhere. I would be pissing for long periods of time. I went from weighing one hundred fifty pounds to one hundred twenty in like six months. I was still doing me, and drinking syrup wasn't helping it at all. My face had lost roundness and I was starting to look gaunt. All my clothing was too big for me to wear. I was literally going through hell. I chose not to be around anybody who told me anything about taking my medicine. That was how I was at first—a niggah was straight lost.

My second year of having the shit wasn't much better. I stayed sick, going to the hospital, where I always ended up checking myself out. Like an idiot, I was drinking codeine very heavy, not knowing the shit kept my sugar sky-high. I was a regular at the Lady of the Lake hospital. When I'd show up, they would send me right to ICU.

In April of 2005, my lil niggah Ivy was gunned down in cold blood. During that time, my health was at its all-time worst condition. I was drinking two to three pints of syrup on a regular basis. Hell, I was taking straight shots out the bottle. I remember one day my niggah Bleek was telling me I needed to go check into a hospital for a while, being I had lost so much weight. He kept telling me, "Don't worry about nothing. I'ma hold the block down while you're in recovery." He was right too. I needed some help, but all I could think about was my boy being gone and never coming back.

The next day I ended up getting in a car crash. My shit was totaled. Bleek got arrested, which only made the shit worse. My body felt like it was going to shut down. I was drained and felt lightheaded. I checked my blood sugar and the meter indicated it was high. I needed to lie down and take some of the stress off my body, but I had to tend to my man. After I bonded Bleek out, I decided to head to the hospital because I was starting to get sick. Once they checked my blood sugar, it read 685. (Normal is less than 140.) I was down to one hundred twenty pounds.

In all actuality, I was dying. I was unable to tend to my own needs, so they kept me in the hospital for about two weeks. My first week was spent in ICU, and the second week I was moved to a room until I wasn't in DKA (diabetic ketoacidosis) anymore. I was fucked up, in very bad shape. Ivy hadn't liked it when I drank so much codeine, so to honor him and make him proud, I chose to stop drinking syrup. By the time I was released from the hospital, I was feeling good.

After six months of lying up and doing nothing, I was back tripping again. I hated it when people would come to see me in the hospital, but I have to admit, the nurses were extra nice to me. They always gave me a room at the end of the hall and didn't allow people to bother me. They checked up on me on a regular basis and made sure I was comfortable during my stay.

After being released, I decided to write a song regarding my situation. The song was called "I Quit." It would be a reminder of what the drank had done to my body and my reason for stopping. When I relapsed at times, all I could think about was the part in the song when I said, *One sip led to ten and now I'm on that drank again . . .*

In 2007, I was recovering very well. In fact, I was a hell of lot better. Unfortunately, I was still drinking lean, but only on certain occasions. I might've visited the hospital maybe once or twice during 2007. My sickness was rather tricky, so while I was in the hospital, to ensure my safety, I began learning more about taking my insulin and how my body operated. I would be lying in a hospital bed in the fetal position, crying and asking God, "Why me?" Tears soaked my bedsheets as I buried my face to contain my sounds of agony. What had I done so bad that it had brought me to that point? Even though hospitals had saved my life on several occasions, I still didn't like them. Being in front of, inside, or on your way to the hospital only meant something was wrong.

There were times I needed to go to the hospital and I would totally refuse, but Nita would be on my ass. She didn't play that shit. To be honest, I think she took my health more seriously than I did. If she happened to see a change in my condition, she'd practically demand that I go see a doctor, even if she had to take drastic measures like dragging me out the house. She'd be like, "Boosie, get up and let's go. You need to seek professional help, so come on, and I'm not playing."

I hate to admit it, but she was right. While I was being rebellious and stuck in my pride, I'd end up throwing up all over the room. I would debase the floor, the bed, the bathroom, and myself. If all else failed, she'd grab the phone and call my mom. Without pause, Mom would rush over to my aid, but not without getting in my shit for not listening to Nita.

After enduring the pain for so long, I would give in and tell Nita to call the damn hospital and tell them to get my bed ready. Yeah, you heard right—I had become so regular there, they kept my room available. They would be waiting for me in the emergency room and would go through the same procedure as always to get me back on track. Then I would get out and do good for about six months before relapsing again.

Once in 2008, it was very cold outside and I had a real bad cough. It was one of those times when I knew I needed medical attention. I hated getting a cold while having diabetes because the shit would last so damn long. The crazy thing was, when I had a cough, I never really felt sick, but when I'd check my sugar, the shit would read high. Immediately, I would go and get a checkup. Sometimes the doctor would tell me I had to remain under their care because I had pneumonia. I wasn't doing any hard drugs at the time, so I would be like, "Damn, I can't win for losing." And once again I'd spend about a week in the hospital, stressed out.

Another time after I'd gotten out of the ICU, I checked myself out of the hospital. I immediately caught a plane to Michigan to make a concert. It was a must—had I not gone, the promoter would have stuck me with a lawsuit. Even though I only had forty percent of my voice and forty percent of my strength, I still went and performed one hundred percent.

In prison, my diabetes was an issue. Sometimes I would be afraid to fall asleep because I was on extended lockdown with no cell mate, so if my sugar dropped, there would be no one there to save me. In those cases, I just stayed up all night and slept all day. Also, the prison doctors weren't very good. I felt that due to us being inmates, the doctors' concern for our well-being was less than it would be for a regular person on the street. I prayed daily that my diabetes wouldn't be a curse on my children. I wouldn't wish that sickness on my worst enemy.

When I got my freedom, I wanted to address the issue of kids suffering from juvenile diabetes and how important it is for them to take care of themselves. There are so many people in the world living with sicknesses and don't even know it. I do know this: it has been a helluva fight, and to this day, I'm still fighting the disease. With the diabetes, I would always be so close to dying, but I would always come back. I would come back, recover, then make a CD. I always made songs about my struggles in life, whether it was about my hospital visits, my time in prison, or the loss of a loved one. I took my diabetes like a man and it made me stronger.

Even my music would become stronger, since my situation would give me more of my own life story to be creative around. I didn't see it back then, but my diabetes would help me to become a better person.

One time I remember going into a diabetic coma and having to be rushed to the hospital. I was taken to the same room my father had died in. I didn't really know it until I awakened. My mother said, "Do you know this is the same room your father died in?" Was my mother trying to give me a warning? I didn't really know what to say to that.

■ ■ ■

I know some people would have collapsed under the weight of all that I've been through. In some ways, I feel God has placed a light on me to make other people stronger. I have always felt that way. When I was diagnosed with diabetes, others around me felt they could beat it also, knowing the person they looked up to was surviving the same ailment. When I went through those types of things, it gave other people hope.

Currently, my day-to-day is waking up and exercising. I'm trying to keep my sugar at a respectable level. That's what I'm basically doing. The more I work out, the fewer diabetic meds I have to take. That's something I have to face with all the stress I'm going through just fighting this diabetes. Just having this sickness is a pain. It's not easy—I can't say that at all. I wake up like a soldier and fight the shit every day, knowing the more I work out, the better I become. I'm still fighting it, though.

Right now, I'm insulin-dependent. Even though I exercise, it's still a struggle because I want to eat certain things. Sometimes I can get hardheaded with it. I try to eat, then work out. Then when I get home, I try to satisfy all my cravings. When I want it, I want it now. I want to try something new, like a Pop-Tart or some shit like that. I would work out and do everything right, but at the end of the day, I'd still want some watermelon. A lot of times, I find myself doing things that are not that healthy for me. I guess that's what comes with being Boosie Badazz—I'm trying but I'm not perfect.

Chapter 14

CANCER– THE ENEMY WITHIN ME

The thing I went through with cancer really gave people hope. When God flashed that light on me, others were saying, "Well, Boosie, you have cancer and I also have it. With all that you've been through, I feel as though I can beat it."

When I was fighting my murder charge, I'd had doubts about victory even though I knew I wasn't guilty. Those doubts were caused by the media, who were against me. But with the cancer, it wasn't between me and the media, or the police, or a judge. I knew this was between me and God. With a good legal team, I could fight the system—but cancer was something different. There was no amount of money that could promise recovery. It was only my will to live, along with the power of prayer. Cancer was in my family bloodline; my aunt Keisha and my aunt Jean had both died from it. I had been close with both of them. Everyone I knew who had cancer was dying. It was sort of making me have second thoughts, and sometimes I wondered if I had finally entered my last battle.

It was a hard fight knowing the damage that cancer can do to a person. But I wasn't giving up; I just couldn't. I had a lot of life left and a lot to live for. I was at a crossroads between my subconscious and my heart. At night, I would pray to God, but in my head, I would wonder if I was going to pull through. Death was right before me and I felt its presence. The day after being diagnosed with cancer, I saw everything I had done in life flash before my eyes.

I was losing hope at that moment. I was still praying, but the hope was fading. My prayers came because this voice in my mind kept saying, "With faith as small as a mustard seed . . ." So that's what kept my prayer going. I was losing so much weight that it began scaring me. I continued to work on my body and mind. I think that's why some people die from cancer: stressing. You gotta keep people who are going through that illness happy. Sometimes all I could say was, "Really, God? It's over with, just like that?"

The way I had gotten the diagnosis was that my sugar was high, so I thought I was in DKA. In the hospital they found a spot on my stomach and my kidney, so the doc wanted to check it out. When they did an X-ray of my stomach, the results came back that I had cancer. I had renal cell carcinoma in my right kidney. The doc informed me that an immediate surgery had to be done. I damn near went into a panic attack. I had already reached stage two, so shit was serious. I had to remember that the doctors were professionals and they'd done the procedure many times. I had to have faith in their work.

I'm talking about, a niggah was going through it. I was stressed out. I started selling everything. I was panicking, not knowing what I was facing. I was selling my cars and jewelry—I mean, everything. I thought my life was over for sure. I used to have nightmares, especially in the week leading up to my surgery. I was having all sorts of bad dreams. I was fucked up in the head. The crazy thing was, when I dreamed or had nightmares, I could never remember them. It was like two or three dreams in my head at the same time. Crazy, right? The cancer was really working on me. The shit had me scared.

I ended up having to pay for my surgery. The shit came out to be like ninety-six thousand dollars due to the fact that I didn't have insurance. I didn't have my shit together. I didn't know the importance of insurance until then. The sickness was really putting a dent in my pockets. When it first came to their attention that I was going to pay by check, I guess that wasn't what they wanted to hear. They told me it would take two to three months to get the surgery. When I told them I could pay in cash, immediately they bumped it to a week. I didn't know what to expect. It was hard looking at myself. I had never been so little in my life.

I went and had my surgery at the MD Anderson Cancer Center on December 8, 2015. On my way to the hospital, I had smoked a joint and the shit had me loaded. The weed had a niggah tripping—

I couldn't stop smiling and laughing to myself. I kept thinking about some shit that had happened a couple of days prior. The funny thing was, I believe the doctor knew I was high. I called myself soaking my body with cologne and lotion, but I still think they smelled the shit. I ended up getting admitted the same day as my surgery.

I felt good and it wasn't just from the weed. My mother was there to support me through it all. She was accompanied by my kids. A few of my homies were there for me as well. There were a lot of people all across the world sending out their prayers for me. All I cared about were those who were there for me, but after receiving so much love, I almost melted. I had God on my side. It's just that my faith wasn't all the way there.

The shit was life-changing: sitting and watching others lying on the floor, dying. I was at the point of feeling like I wasn't going to make it. What separated me from those other people? What made my situation any different from theirs? They were dying, so why should I survive? I got to thinking back to when two of my aunts had died, not to mention one of my uncles. People all around me were dying of cancer. My uncle Kenny, my daddy's brother—his was the most recent death. So you can see why, when the shit hit me, I was like, *I guess it might be my time to go too.*

When the doctor administered that gas, it put me right to sleep. I was out for hours, but it seemed like only minutes. The shit felt awesome. I think it was like a four-hour procedure, something like that. During the surgery, they removed thirty percent of my right kidney. At least I still have some of my kidney left. I had a great doctor and he did an amazing job on me.

I remember waking up from my surgery and I was feeling a little pain. My doctor was standing over me, looking down. He said, "I told you, you were going to blink your eyes and everything would be all over with." Then he asked me, "Do you do concerts every night?"

I told him, "Yeah. That's what I do on a day-to-day basis. In my career, I have done over two thousand of them." He informed me that from that day on, I'd have to be more careful and start thinking about my future, possibly one without music. *Life without music? This niggah can't be serious*, I thought. Music was my life. It was how I maintained, how I breathed—music defined me. It was my way of expression and the communication link between me and the world. I couldn't leave that behind. Hell, I was really just getting started.

After the surgery, I had to learn how to walk again. My legs were as useless as a baby's for five days. Once I did regain control of my legs, I had to use a walker. I had to do my rehab for two months or so, but for my first couple of days after the surgery, all I did was rest in my hospital bed. I didn't even bother trying to do anything. My body was worn out and wasn't responding to my brain.

Then I kept seeing people walking past my door, staring all in my room and shit. Everybody was walking in circles around the place. I would see people standing in a line walking, patients walking with their nurses. People were coming up to me saying "You want to go for a walk?" and I would be like "No." Then I finally got up and said, "Fuck this shit! I gotta get up off my ass and start walking if I ever want to have access to my legs again."

One day after a week of being in the hospital, I woke up and saw there was a walker by my bedside. I had this song in my head and I wanted to get it out before I ended up forgetting it. With only a little strength, I prayed that God see me through what I was about to do. With much struggle, I was able to clothe myself. I took hold of the walker and snuck out the hospital to go to the studio. I made it there safely, but every time I tried to rap, a sharp pain would pierce my side. I was going through hell, but I was determined to get the job done. I ended up recording a whole CD using a walker to balance me in the booth.

Rehab was what really helped me get through. Four to five hours a day of training got me back together. I was an outpatient, so I always had to go to the facility for my workout. When I left rehab, I would head straight to the studio. My doctor changed my walker to the kind you can sit on, so when I was in the booth I would sit on it. The producers used to bring the mic down to my level, and I'd just sit there and rap.

I knew I was going to be all right. The doctor told me I would have to use the walker for about three weeks, for safety reasons. It would take some time for me to get my strength back. He explained that it mainly came with patience. I believed him, and besides, I'm a fighter. I wasn't tripping though. As long as the shit didn't kill me, it would only make me stronger. I used the walker for three and a half weeks like the doc had ordered. After breakfast, I would take about an hour walk. I repeated that cycle after lunch and likewise supper.

I needed to take it easy, and sleep was essential. The good thing was I pretty much stopped having those bad dreams when I returned home from the hospital. I figured it was from being in that medical environment. I was around nothing but white coats that resembled angels to me, and that caused the nightmares to manifest. At home in my own environment, I was comfortable and more relaxed. But being up, hustling, and chasing that money for two or three days at a time with no rest brought the dreams back into my life. I think it was God telling me to slow my ass down and realize that money ain't everything. I couldn't help it though; that was my lifestyle. I was bad at sleeping. I probably slept maybe two to three hours a day. Like I said, I was fucked up. I do still extend my love for MD Anderson hospital in Houston, Texas. They're the best cancer hospital ever, like, in the world.

■ ■ ■

I know the only reason I beat cancer was because of God. So many people die from cancer, and there I was: still living and functional. I think God was trying to get my attention, you know? I think that was His way of humbling me, like He was saying, *I have gotten you through the storm, brought you home, and gave you all this. Now it's your time to give back.* That's what brought me back to the realization that He has the last say. Yeah, that was God making me real-ize something: He could have taken me at any time, but He chose not to. He still has a purpose left for me to fulfill.

Since then I've gotten much stronger. I talk better, walk better, and breathe better. I even believe that the increase of my success came from those struggles. The blessings were buried inside them. I weathered the struggles with His strength to regain my own. They say there's three levels of a storm: you're either entering a storm, going through a storm, or coming out of a storm. But we shouldn't focus on the storm, because there's a blessing that awaits us on the other side.

I've struggled all of my life, but cancer was a struggle like no other. Even though I'd fought with diabetes, there was no compari-son. I was able to deal with the diabetes, but cancer, that shit was on a whole other level of sickness. That shit ain't even from this world.

I want all cancer survivors to know how lucky we are. No, scratch that—I want all my cancer survivors to know how blessed we are, how loved and appreciated. God reached out His right hand and snatched us back before Satan could fully wrap his arms around us. Through His stripes, God's Son paid the price for our healing; that's how much God loves us. Realizing the ultimate sacrifice that was made so I could live, there will never be a doubt in my heart of what He can and will do if we obey His Word. When you're God's child, He is on your side.

A lot of people didn't receive these blessings. Many died facing off with this demon known as cancer. I've bumped into many people on the streets and received plenty of fan mail from people who have run into this unchained beast. They say, "Boosie, I just want you to know your cancer song saved my life," or "Boosie, I just want you to know you gave me hope when I was fighting cancer." We've all shared the same pain and prayers, so we know how the others feel.

I'd been around people with cancer before I was diagnosed with it, but that's two different sides of the field. You don't know how that person feels or the thoughts that trample through their mind. Their mind is not operating like the mind of a healthy person. To put it bluntly, even if you were caring for and nursing a cancer patient for years, you cannot fully relate to their pain or struggles. Unless you have experienced it, you could never imagine this pain. Now that I've been on both sides, I can relate.

Chapter 15

FATHERHOOD

This is who I do it for: family.

L ooking at this world through my eyes, I would have to say, the best joy in life is being a father. I look at it like a professional sport and I always try to be MVP every year. Being a father is different from being a mother. Mothers will always be loved. It's more like an honor being a father, especially when the kid runs past Mom and leaps into your arms.

I love being a dad. I love to see the smiles my kids give me, their respect and appreciation. They're the sole reason I want more out of life. They give me that extra drive I need to be successful, so they are a big part of who I am today. If you've ever listened to my music or watched any of my DVDs, you can see and feel the joy I get out of being a daddy.

I cannot understand how a man can walk out on his child, never to return. How some leave no trace of their existence at all. That eats me up inside. I have no respect for a man of that nature.

Much of the time, the damaged blueprints left from our parents get passed down the generations. Sometimes as parents we encounter certain situations, and we tend to think we handled them well—not realizing a wave caused by our parents passed over us and impacted our children. We have to realize that the dumb shit we do could become a curse to our seeds and to their seeds as well.

Fatherhood for me all started when Walnita told me she was pregnant. At first, I couldn't believe it. I think my heart missed a few beats. The next nine months changed me for real. Finally, on December 4, 2001, Iviona Hatch was born at Woman's Hospital. Your boy was a daddy. I was there through it all. I watched as her little bitty head was just going in and out, in and out. After giving her mother so much hell, she finally popped out and stayed out. She was a fat, cute little baby. I was so happy I didn't know how to act. I felt like the luckiest man on Earth.

When we brought her to settle into her new home, I had no idea how to hold or handle a baby. I didn't know you had to support her head. I was still learning. She was a good little baby, though. I remember one time I called myself trying to change her diaper. My momma kept telling me, "Wait, boy. She might not be done yet." Thinking I knew everything, I wiped her down and was trying to make her laugh and smile. I was holding her high above my head without her diaper on, and what do you know? My little girl boo-

booed all over my chest and neck. My momma and Nita both broke out in laughter. That was a hilarious moment—for them.

When Iviona was two years old, she had this thing she did with her eyes, and we called it sweet eyes. She would blink her eyes when I would say, "Give Daddy sweet eyes." When she was young, everywhere I went, she would run behind me, crying and tugging at my clothes. She was a real daddy's girl.

Iviona is multitalented. She loves sports, fashion, and music. That little girl loves her family dearly. She's an excellent listener and she gets straight As in school. That's my little princess. She never missed a visit to come see me. One thing I can say for sure is she loves her daddy.

My second child's name is Tylayja Hatch. We nicknamed her Pretty Black. She's ten months younger than Iviona, by a different mother. During the first year of her life, we didn't have a relationship because her mom and I were always beefing with one another. When I used to go by to get her, she would always cry when I picked her up. I knew it was only because she wasn't familiar with me. Once she got used to me, she wouldn't want to go home. Just like her sister, she is a straight-A student. She loves to dress, run track, and cheerlead. Also like her sister, she's fond of music.

One thing about Ty is she loves to ask questions. She is the shy type, but if she's around people she feels comfortable with, she can get really loose. It's easier to get tears out of her than Iviona because Ty is a sensitive child, very delicate. She loves being around her family, and if someone speaks negative about her daddy, best believe she's coming to tell me. She loves coming to see her daddy and spend time with me. That's my Pretty Black. She is something else. When we're alone, we love to talk and laugh about all kinds of things.

My third child's name is Torrence Hatch Jr. He's eleven months younger than Ty, by a third woman. When he was a baby, he used to cry and shit all over the place. That little niggah was something else. He used to give me the blues. When he called himself flashing out on me, I used to drop his ass off at my aunt Jean and cousin Tash's house. By the time he was three years old, we were calling him Too-tie Badazz because the little niggah was a bad muthafucka. He loves to dress, get money, and play football. Most of all, he wants to be a rapper just like his daddy.

Torrence knows more and has seen more than most kids his age. Growing up, he used to mimic everything I did, so a lot of his ways came from me. He's not as bad as he used to be; he's settled down a lot. The little niggah can recite my songs word for word, and he really takes pride in being around his family. One thing I can say about him is he loves his brothers and sisters. Also, my little man loves cars. He's an addict when it comes to go-karts. Growing up, he's taken more ass-whippings than any of my kids, but he means well. He's a good kid with a big heart.

I would love for my son to be in the music industry, because I know about the business and how to make money in it. I'm well plugged with the connects, so if my kids turn to music, I'm here for them. Whoop-whoop, let's print that album and get that money!

All my kids are incredibly talented, gifted beyond my expectations. As a father, I would never force my kids in the direction of music, but if they choose it, I'm sending them to *American Idol* tomorrow.

I used to tell my grandma I wanted ten kids. Still to this day, I want ten kids. Anybody who knows me will tell you that, over the years, I kind of have been planning it out in my heart. I loved coming from a large extended family and I wanted to carry that on. Now that I'm a father, I find myself trying to provide my children with all the things in life my parents couldn't afford to buy me, making sure they get to places in the world they might want to visit.

One thing I often notice my disciplinary actions is that are similar to my father's. I see myself raising my kids in the same fashion in which he raised my brother and me. Some might say I raise them hard, and I would probably agree with that. I used to beat their asses, just like Daddy used to do to us. You know, the kind of ass-whipping you got that you remembered years on down the line. Daddy didn't play: when it was ass-whipping time, he got straight to the point. I know what it did for me, so I knew it would work for my kids as well.

What the shit did was put fear into my heart. When I was in school and decided to do some fucked-up shit, images of Daddy would flash across my mind and that shit would put me right back in gear. That's what I wanted to instill in my kids. My dad told me that fear only evolves into respect if applied properly.

My father hated the law and so did we. Naturally, I'm raising my kids to hate the police, just like their grandfather and daddy.

They know cops are supposed to be here to serve and protect, but the majority of them don't follow that code. They're here to serve their interests and protect their own.

As a man, I knew how to raise my boys. It was the girls I had no knowledge about. With them, I just went with the flow of things.

My kids were all born in a cycle. Like I explained earlier, it's Ivionia (Ivy), then Pretty Black; she was ten months after Ivy. When I hooked up with her mom, we were out of the same hood. I had my son Torrence, who was born ten months after her, which leads us to my other daughter, Toriana, who was born ten months after him.

One thing about my children and me is we love spending time together. We love having talks with one another and sharing secrets. We dine, shop, and listen to music together. They aren't perfect, but they are amazing children, and I commend them for their efforts. This light of mine only shines through them. Even though they're kids, I can easily lean on them if I have something on my chest. I feel as if I can tell them anything, so I'd like to start by telling Ivy, my oldest daughter, about her father. One day I want to sit down one-on-one with her and explain that her father has done some things for her that were not good; things that I am not now nor will I ever be proud of. Things I can never take back, but that had to be done at the time.

The things I did after having my first two or three kids were done in survival mode. I had to make moves and not just for me, but for my family also. Daddy was dead. I had to be the man of the house, even if I wasn't living there. Decisions had to be made, and every step had to vibrate the concrete.

My first year of making those moves was based on the question: When am I going to stand up and be a real boss? When am I going to make the sacrifices needed to get real money? I knew if I didn't, life was going to be hard on my people, and I didn't want that. I wanted the best for them. I felt I either had to hit these streets or sit back and watch my people starve to death.

So, to my first three kids: Daddy had to do a lot of things. All of that came from standing up to people, having the will to get up and do overtime on the hustle, staying up until the cocks crowed, and enduring even further than that. I think back on the nights I didn't sleep, and the only images and thoughts parading through my mind were those of my kids: what they meant to me and how my decisions could alter our lives.

I want Ivy to know that all those late nights away from home were for her benefit. There was no way I could watch my first three kids inherit the pains and struggles of the life I had coming up. No offense to my parents and the excellent effort they put forth—I give it all to them. At the same time, it was hard with my first three because that was right after my dad died, so I had hella pressure on me. I just felt like my kids deserved better.

I would tell Tylayja that no matter how much her mom and I had confrontations, it never affected the love I carry for her. Her mother and I have different viewpoints, and sometimes that affects a daughter's relationship with her father, but I wasn't letting that happen with me and T. That was the thing with her mother: that woman loves an argument. You know how women are: they get to throwing shit all around the house, then call the police and tell them you did it. I know those arguments frightened my daughter at times, and that's why I would just leave. Daddy loves you, Princess. I would tell all my kids that, even though they heard differently from their mothers, especially my second child.

Now, for my son Tooter, I would tell him like this, and this is a quote from one of my songs, "Even if Mommy tells you something different, Daddy loves you dearly. Mommy and Daddy go through difficult situations at times, which leads to a lot of arguing and yelling. That's life. That's the reality of being in a relationship."

I know it was hard for my offspring because they had to grow up at a time when their mothers and I were separated. Knowing their moms, I know they had a lot of negative shit to say about me, mainly in front of my children. I hustled so hard because I had to show them that Daddy loves them unconditionally. I had to go extra, extra hard for my second and third children. For Iviona, I was there the whole time; you know, she went through it with me. My second and third kids, I was only there intermittently. It was sometimes a mess having my first three children born all having different mothers. Nita was always cool when it came to the children because she felt they were all innocent and didn't ask to be in the world. But Tylayja and Torrence always had to go back home to their mothers when they'd visit because of the bullshit they kicked up. That was the main issue having kids by different women. Favoritism was not my thing when it came to my children, but try explaining that to a bitter baby-momma. I was lucky with my baby girl Iviona, who stayed up under me the whole time. She didn't have to go anywhere because Nita and I were a couple at the time. Eventually, when my second and third ones came over, they stayed more often. Tooter was there the most. He used to love to come by. That little niggah was horrible. So when Tylayja and Tooter came, I would try my best to pour out all my love to them.

I never wanted my second and third children to go home. I wanted them to stay, so when they did, I would just flood them with love. I did that because of how their mommas were, but I had to be careful. Even though we weren't together, there was still a lot of friction. The friction kept the kids and me at a distance at times, but when I had the kids, I didn't hesitate to express my love for them. I would tell them, "Daddy did so much for y'all. I did so much to bring y'all together to share your love with one another." My first three know what Daddy did for them.

Many nights I cried to myself, thinking about them and how I felt so empty without them when they weren't around. Just as I expressed my love for them, they needed to do the same for each other. That was the sweetest time in life for me, doing what I had to do to get them all together. I needed them all to know each other. None of them should be in the dark about who their siblings are. When they got older, I didn't have to explain that to them; they already knew the work I'd put in and the blame I'd taken just to make things right.

Through all of that, to this day, they are close-knit. That's because I refused to give up. Looking back on them now, I feel I did a damn good job of uniting them and teaching them how to love one another. Even if their mothers didn't get along, I went through the obstacles for those kids. I did everything I could for them. They needed to know that no matter what, Daddy's gonna be there. That was mainly for the older ones. My youngest ones, Michael and Laila Jean, didn't have any issues because they were around me so much, it automatically showed. They know my love is unconditional. I don't separate them or love one more than the next. They all are my world.

By me not having my kids with me every day, I had to prove myself. The ones that lived with me got a chance to feel Daddy's compassion firsthand. The others didn't reside in my home, so I would just get them on holidays and weekends; you know, things of that nature. I wanted them to know that even though Daddy wasn't there daily, my love for them still flowed nonstop. In fact, it flowed more because I missed them so much. I'd tell them Daddy was working hard to provide for them and missing them like crazy.

Along with my children, I also do for a few others. I have to make sure I'm there for my partner Bleek's daughter, Emari, and a couple more. I provide for them because their fathers aren't there, and I believe they would do the same for me. As a friend, that's what

I have to do. In my eyes, it's only right. My heart is open like that. Plus, those who were good to me, I will never forget them.

I have to make sure my kids are well taken care of. I have to make sure they never hold their hands out to another person, asking for anything. I have to make sure they know life and the seriousness of it and how to accept the good with the bad. They need to know that life has obstacles and be prepared for them.

If I didn't have any kids, I wouldn't have to work so hard, especially while dealing with my diabetes and cancer. Like I said, my kids are the only reason I grind—I gotta make sure they are straight. I can't think about getting just a million dollars. Hell naw, that shit has to be split eight ways. I have to be thinking more like eight million, so they can get at least a million apiece. I have to come home and build an empire per month for my family. I'm a street niggah and that's what I have to do.

I don't really judge the word "love" anymore. I can't because people love you for entirely different reasons. Unconditional love is what I give my children. It's just everything to me. It's past my budget, it doesn't matter to me. I would go in the hole for my children. It's not just about material things; it's changing diapers, movie nights on Tuesdays, poem nights on Wednesdays. That shit is bigger than money.

When you have money, you want to take your kids to the theme parks at least three, four times a month. If you've got money like that, you have to turn that shit into love. We go to water parks, Six

Flags, Great America, the Dells, all that. Living like that will make my kids want to have money when they are older, so they can do the same for their kids.

That comes with discipline also. You gotta beat their asses when needed, because if you don't, they will easily stray. I raised my kids by playing with them all the time, but when they got out of line, I put my foot down. They knew the seriousness of my love, but they also knew I didn't play the bullshit games. Kids can sometimes get beside themselves. As they get older, they'll try balling up their fists to you; they'll try to talk back and puff up at you. That's why you have to discipline them while they are young.

I was raised that you spare the rod, you spoil the child. It's not really on the mothers; it's really on the fathers. I say that simply because the mother already nurtures. They do that from birth, so it's the father's job to beat their kids' asses. My mom, she didn't really put her hands on me. I can remember maybe one or two times she might've slapped me up. She would just put me in the corner and make me read books and shit. Now, as far it went with Daddy, he didn't play that shit at all. I knew if I did something I shouldn't, I was getting my ass whipped. If a child doesn't have that kind of discipline, they will eventually wild out.

When my daddy died, I was thinking, *Now who's going to tell me the things I need to know?* That's why daddies need to be in their kids' lives as much as mothers are. I know it isn't the father's fault all the time, but if you're not in that child's life, their brain will malfunction in some sort of way. That's what all the fathers need to know. Fuck what the momma is doing, we as men have to take the initiative for the well-being of the children. Trust, abandoning your child will definitely fuck up their head.

While I was in prison, I literally made dudes reach out to their kids. I'd always tell them not to give up, just get it right. Even though you're in jail, you still have to work to build that relationship with them. Being in jail makes it harder, but you have to start somewhere. I know it will be hard sometimes, because sometimes the mothers are trying to stop us, but we can't give up; we gotta keep trying. One day when you come back to the table with your son or daughter, you're going to say, "Look, I know I've made some mistakes, but look at all the things Daddy tried to do to be a part of your life." We have to do that because eventually, the truth will come to light.

I raised my kids to have hope and believe in themselves and each other. Now, that's big. I've got one of my daughters trying the face cream business; I have another daughter and my son doing the rap thing. They all are involved in something. I'm just trying to keep it going. That's what it's all about for me. I just try to spread the energy—you know, build a people who are bigger than Boosie. The same goes for the children; they're bigger than Boosie.

Fatherhood is being there for your children. A father should do all the special things for his children, like taking the kids on their first trip, being present during any event they might have going on, and giving them the talk on the birds and the bees. A father basically sets the stage for his kids, whereas a daddy doesn't necessarily do things like that. Like, I had a daddy who was also a father. Daddies are absent a lot. They're the ones who have every excuse in the world. My father did take the time to sit me down and have those fatherly talks with me. I have eight kids of my own and two other kids I adopted. The two who are adopted belong to my two best friends, Ivy and Bleek, who both were killed. Bleek's daughter, Emari, and Ivy's little boy named after him have become part of my tribe.

When my boy Ivy got killed, it happened like this: We were at the club partying, doing our thing. Some hating-ass niggaz got on some funny shit with my niggah, but we deadened that shit immediately— at least we thought we did. The shit died down, so we continued fuckin' with bitches. After it was all over, we left and gathered together by the cars. We made our plans for the remainder of the night, got in the cars, and headed out. Ivy was in the car with some of our other guys, while Bleek was in the car with me. Ivy and the guys in the vehicle with him were about one hundred feet in front of us. No one in either car was paying attention to our surroundings, so we had no idea the sky was about to fall.

From out of nowhere, a car pulls up alongside Ivy and them. "Who the fuck is that?" I said. Before anyone could answer, the vehicle was spraying so many bullets into the car Ivy was in, I couldn't believe my eyes. "Go, go, go, go! Get them niggaz!" I yelled. As we were pulling up, the other car was pulling off. We were about to chase them and gun them down, but we had to make sure our people were straight first. When I approached their car, I couldn't believe what I was seeing. I couldn't believe they had taken my partner. Naw, not my boy. They had just murdered Ivy. They had taken the lives of everyone inside the vehicle. The shit was crazy. I couldn't believe it.

All I could do was pace the pavement trying to make sense of the shit. Who the fuck were those niggaz and where did they come from? What I did know was that I wanted revenge. I wanted those niggaz to pay for what they did. Someone had to answer for that loss. Someone had to be held responsible. Not just for me, but for the sake of Ivy's family. I had to get my thinking in order though. That was a time I had to step up for the greater good.

At the time, Ivy's girl was pregnant with his son. That was my fuckin' boy, so I felt it was only right that I be there. That's how I was raised, and it was a calling. It's just what I was called to do.

Now, my boy Bleek—the same shit happened to my niggah. He got murdered a couple of months after I went to jail, so, likewise, it's my duty to be there for his daughter. Sure enough, she calls me Daddy, and I know my niggah wouldn't have it any other way. At the same time, she knows who her father was. I would never take that from her, or any of them for that matter. We were like that. We made promises to each other. I told him, if I ever died, then it was his duty to raise my kids. He in turn said the exact same thing to me. There you have it: a pact was made and that goes for all my dogs. It's always been like that. If you're my homie and I fucks with you the long way, then it's my duty to care and provide for your seed.

I love these two dearly. I'm just trying to fill that void in their lives. I don't go to the malls for my kids unless they are included. What I really do is constantly remind them that their daddies were the shit. I always try to motivate them by telling them stories about their fathers. I tell them everything about how great they were, how good they were to me, and how they were always there for me. They love when I tell them those stories. They be like, "Hey, what did my daddy use to do?" So I tell them stories to motivate them.

All of my kids call them their sister and brother. They don't look at them any differently than their biological sisters and brothers. When you really love somebody, you do shit like that. It's just a call to duty. Both of the kids' mothers love me. They have a deep respect for me for stepping up to the plate. They would say, "I wish their daddy had more friends like you." They always tell me things like that. On many occasions, they have said, "Let me cook you something to eat. Are you hungry?" I would respond, "Naw, I'm good, but thank you though." That's just how it was. They are honored to have me in their kids' lives and I am honored to be here. I would never fuck up the opportunity to be in their lives. Just like Ivy, Bleek, and I were one, their seeds are one with my own.

Chapter 16

SUPERHERO

My cousin, who I always call my little sister,
getting married to one of my workers.

When I first came out, everybody wanted to sound like Boosie. They wanted that swag and that image; it was like the whole area was trying to be like me. The shit was crazy. I was out here making plenty of moves, and when I came out with the song "What About Me," the shit hit bigger than I'd thought.

That was the record I dropped right before I caught my deal. It had people going crazy, hollerin' out, "I smoke, I drank." I wrote the record because I was saying, you know, they signed all these other rappers but I was feeling like, *Shit, they ain't Boosie.* I was feeling like I knew I was a superhero from the love I got, the respect, and the smiles on the kids' faces when they saw me.

I remember one time I took two of my partners with me to Baton Rouge, and they were amazed at how the little kids there would walk up to me and just stare at me. They saw how I was giving back to my community, how I would round up all the kids and take them to get their hair cut when I was down there. I would gather up all the little girls and take them to the beauty shop and get their fingernails and toes done. I'd take them out to eat.

They were surprised at the amount of love and protection I received while we were down there. All the kids would gather around me, saying, "Boosie, Boosie, we love you, Boosie." Some called me their big brother or even their father. People would come to tears when they saw me. The older people would even get out of their cars and lay hands on me. They were proud of me, being where I'd come from. They love me, man, and I love the fact that they do.

On holidays I would do something special for all the kids in the neighborhood. On Christmas, I showed up and gave out gifts like I was Santa Claus. On Thanksgiving, I gave out turkeys like I was the government. Everybody would be lined up because they knew Boosie was coming and bearing gifts. On Easter, I would give out like a thousand bikes. The shit was in my heart, it's just who I am. Every holiday, kids knew there was a chance they might not receive anything from their parents—but they knew they had something coming from Boosie. I didn't do it to knock the parents; naw, I did it as a shoulder to lean on. I love my people, and my heart, door, and finances are always open to the less fortunate.

This went on for five years before I was sent to prison. I always gave back to the hood. That's what made me the Robin Hood of the ghetto, man. I never took from the hood, only gave back.

Right now, I'm trying to give back to as many as I can and save as many as I can. If you were close to me and you've passed, the shit hurts me because I feel that maybe there was something I could have done to save you. I'm at the point where if I see people who have lost all hope, I try my best to help them. I just moved one of my nephews in with me, then another nephew. I have to move them in; I have to save them from these streets. My purpose was to move them out of Baton Rouge, because if they ended up dying, I didn't want it to be my fault.

I look back on life now and I'm so glad God took the time to help me and then instilled in my heart the desire to help others. If I can help someone, I will never hesitate to do so. I feel as if I'm chosen to grab people and help them out in any way I can. If I don't do it, I feel like shit; you understand what I'm saying?

That's why, whenever I go back, it's always a celebration. I don't want to think about the past. It's behind me and I want it to stay there. I don't want to think about the dark days, the cold nights, the struggles, and the pain. I don't want people who went through those times to think about those things. I don't even want their relatives to think about them. That's why, when I go back, I try to make it all love. I try to ease the pain or at least make them forget about it. I just want to give and receive love.

It's important to have heroes in our communities because they are the ones who make us believe. That's what the ghetto heroes do: they give you hope. They even make you believe more than some athletes do because you can see them with your own eyes. When you meet these ghetto heroes, you're able to see ten thousand dollars in their pockets right then and there. It's like a movie, but it's right in your face, and shit like that can give you hope. At the same time, it's the wrong hope because you know how they got it.

But at the same time, they make us believe we can be somebody. *If he did it, hell, I can do it* is the thought process. I've had many kids walk up to me and tell me I gave them the strength to do it: "Look, Boosie; look where I came from. It was you who gave me the strength to grind and get it like this." I call myself a ghetto hero because I feel like I've been through so much and every time, God keeps His hands on me. There have been more than six or seven times I should have departed this world, but He forbids it. Every time, I seem to come back much stronger than before, and I capitalize off what I've been through. I give hope to so many people. When you mention Boosie, everybody thinks about their struggles and how to get to the top. I'm here to motivate people.

Everything I say is knowledge if you look at it from a hood point of view. You know what I'm saying? I give it to them in the raw, but it's all knowledge. I'm not telling the kids don't go to school. Hell naw! You'd never hear me say shit like that. I always tell them to go to school. In some songs, we might call women bitches, but where I'm from, you treat a queen like a queen and a hoe like a hoe. I'm just straightforward with it because that's how we were raised Cross the Tracks. A queen solidifies herself with one man and holds her niggah down. You know what I'm saying? Those are the ones you treat like a queen.

■ ■ ■

People call me a philosopher all the time. Sometimes they call me a prophet because I say a lot of shit that comes to pass. The shit be crazy. People call me all kinds of things, but I just try to live and be the man I am.

To be a Black man is hard. It's hard to get up off the ground. I just feel like more Black people need to be bosses and obtain a piece of the pie. Stop letting people tell you to go to work. I don't care how much you're getting paid, it's still a nine-to-five. We shouldn't be afraid of becoming entrepreneurs and being family-oriented.

We need to do what other groups do: take over all the stores. We can run our own communities, but it isn't going to happen if everyone is against everyone else—especially the ones with the money. It's like we're running a race when we should be building an empire. You know how it is in the ghetto, everyone cutting each others' throats. We need to get together and be bosses. We need to let go of the hate.

One day I was thinking about being born in the crack era. I think we were so hurt after the civil rights days that we still had some hate left in us. When the white people left us alone, that hate got directed at the people in our own neighborhoods. How are we against one another when we were just fighting together for the right to go to school or eat in public places, shit like that? I figured a lot of people were still mad and then they moved us all into the same area, where the friction kept on building and building. That's what I can see as a real human being trying to look at this story. Like, the white man ain't trying to get me. The Chinese man ain't out here shooting at me. The Arab man ain't looking at me crazy at a concert. It's sad when the race you have to watch yourself around is your own.

Ninety-nine percent of the time it's a Black man who will be the one to kill a rapper. That's just how it is. Niggah, ain't no white man coming around smoking you like John Lennon. Naw, it's the niggah you went to school with, the niggah you grew up with on the block. They don't want to see you be successful in life.

I got a lot of static when I said that when you look at Black-on-Black crime, we are doing the worst. I wasn't saying our whole race is the worst; what I am saying is Blacks kill more Blacks than anyone else. It most likely isn't a white man who's going to be waiting in my house with a gun. Black people are killing each other by the thousands. Personally I love my Black people, men and women. I was saying that *as a people*, we hate each other the most. We don't get together and start businesses and keep our families together and have miles and miles of rich folks. When it comes to crimes against our own people, we have the worst record. I'm always going to say we should do better.

Another topic I think about is that it isn't fair that once a person does their time, they are no longer allowed to vote. Once you go to prison, you aren't looked upon as a real citizen anymore. If I've done the time the state gave to me, why am I not allowed to be a full citizen of that state? What about the things I've done good? What about the things God has forgiven me for?

Usually the only way you can reach success as an ex-convict is to start your own business, because otherwise most people are going to look at you some kind of way. If you go fill out an application, usually you'll only get the bullshit jobs. You're going to be a cook, or work in a retail store or a fast-food joint. When it comes to prison, most people look at you through the lens of a crime they might have in their heads. They look at all ex-cons as rapists and killers. They don't know what you were in for and they don't know your case, but that's just how the world is.

You know, after we do the time, we're not allowed to carry guns. I feel like they're setting us up to get murdered. That's how I actually feel in my heart. If I'm in the rap industry, I should be allowed to have a gun even with thirty-five convictions because my job is the most dangerous job in the world. You let us out, but you won't let us protect our families?

I feel like it's another way to get rid of us. Either we're going to come home and get killed because we can't carry a firearm, or if we're carrying we're going to get charges. That's just to keep the prison system going and going and going, being that it's the profit center for a lot of small towns. So most convicts when they get released are either going back inside or they're going to the grave. If they were allowed to carry registered guns legally, crime would go down, trust me.

I like the saying Black Lives Matter. There are Black people getting killed by the police on a daily basis in Baton Rouge. It's been happening for so long now, and I like that Black Lives Matter is bringing it into the light. When I was eight years old they killed one of the big-time drug dealers in my hood, Panaya Dog. It was the first funeral I ever went to. That shit got swept under the rug and was never mentioned again.

Now that we have cellphones, it isn't so easy anymore. That's why I post to social media whenever a Black person gets killed. I'm going to show these six million people what the fuck you did and I'm going to talk about it. I'm going to make it go viral because you're a dirty muthafucka. You just shot this man in Oakland! Are you for real? You shot him. You just knocked on his damn window and shot the man sitting there. I feel like it's my job as a real one not to let that shit ride.

Chapter 17

BEING A BOSS

Me and Pimpin' Ken in Milwaukee with   Courtesy of Steve Love
Big Stevo (who took this photo).

When Barak Obama started running for president, all I could think about was what 2Pac had said about Black presidents: it would make Black people strong again. That's just how my heart and soul felt. When Obama won, I just felt like he was empowering us as a race of people. Let me keep it real: I wasn't even really into politics. I wasn't even sure what he was changing or why. I was just like, "Hell yeah! We are going to be strong again." It was amazing to see one of our own in the highest ranking position, ready to make a difference. Even though when he got in, I was still paying higher taxes, you feel me? I was basically going along with "Power to the people!"

Obama's presidency didn't really make a difference with artists, or Black people for that matter, that I could see. After the first term, I felt like it was the same shit. My taxes was high as fuck. But when you walk into a boatload of bullshit, all you can do is try to get it back to right. Even though it was hard to see through the mess that Bush left, I feel like Obama did a great job with the country for those eight years.

I feel like he was put in that position to fail, but Obama pulled it off. It was what you wanted to see out of the president. Good kids, a nice woman, and a respectable man. He came into so much mutha-fuckin' debt, but I do feel that he tried. I just didn't see much prog-ress coming from the top.

That's why whenever I talk to people struggling out here trying to figure it out, I often ask them, what is it that they do? I tell them, "Whatever you do, you can be a boss who makes their own way." I get tired of people struggling and making excuses, so I tell them, "Take what you do and be your own boss. If you're good at cleaning your house, then start your own business doing that." I always try to uplift and motivate people to be their own bosses. That's the solution to being sick and tired of being sick and tired.

With the dudes who have been on the streets hustling their whole lives, I try to encourage them to find a way out of that life. Like, find you a Lil Boosie, man. Find you a little niggah that's going hard for the music and sign him—become a manger and CEO. That's what I try to tell them. One thing for certain, two things for sure: these are my people. Something I hate is to see my people struggling.

Before I give someone anything, I gotta talk to them first. If I just give you a handout and don't talk to you, I feel like I'm enabling you. I always try to talk to uplift them with my experiences. I see so many people who've been doing the same thing for the last fifteen to twenty years. It's like ghetto history is certain to repeat itself. The drug game is a vicious cycle of young Black people wanting to find the easy way to the top. There is no such thing as an easy way to the top. Yeah, some get to play hard without working hard, but that is only temporary.

I would also tell people to pray about whatever situation they're going through. You have to pray about it, because prayer really works. When you choose not to put God in your life, He will allow you to stay in certain situations, stuck, until hopefully you acknowledge Him. Sometimes the only thing you have to go on is faith and you just have to call on God; trust me, He'll hear you. These niggaz out here are doing dumb shit and don't ever call on God. Niggaz who feel like they don't need to call on God don't know His Word.

Shit can be rough if you don't believe in yourself. I tell people, just look at me—look at people who have overcome the things you feel like you can't overcome. I love educating the youth when I speak at the schools and prisons. When I was on parole, I used to go speak with the kids in juvenile facilities because kids look up to famous people. I let them know there is still hope, but they have to do right and better themselves. They would say things like "Well, I ain't got this," or "Why I ain't got that? I don't have a way to do it." I would say, "I didn't have YouTube. Now, what do you expect if you keep coming up with bullshit excuses? It's a big world out there. Adapt and adjust." I would just tell them they have to at least try. If you don't try, then nobody will ever hear you. You gotta try.

I let them know, "There are many ways to get your song out. I didn't have a team back then. I used to have to pass out CDs. I had to do it hand to hand. Shit is different now. You can go to YouTube and put your songs on it. It's called social media. What you're doing is making up excuses. You have to try at least." Some people understand.

I could be a muthafucka, but instead I choose to reach out to my people: you have to have it in your heart to grow, and you have to try. You see me, I'm trying. I'm in a billionaire's DMs right now: "Man, let's do a partnership." Just think, if I do that to twenty damn billionaires, all it takes is one to say, "I believe in you, man. Come on, let's do it." If you don't try, you won't succeed.

I've got people talking to me about how they're trying to get an intern job. There must be about thirty-five hundred artists who're getting that money right now. Why didn't you DM them and ask for an internship? Or tell them, "I will work for free for a month or two"? You keep saying, "I want this, I want that," but you didn't try. Technology has opened up many doors for us to go through.

Ladies, if an artist just poked you on Instagram, you know he's on his phone, right? Tell him, "Well, I want to work. I see you're out here shooting a movie. I want to know if I could hold the cameras for you." That's how you get in. Now you're on the set. If somebody sees you working, they might give you a job. That's better than just sitting at a table with your girls, talking about you want an internship. Basically, what I'm saying is, be a boss. You gotta start thinking for yourself.

These muthafuckas got it sweet now. We didn't have all this when I was coming up. I had to start street-level-type marketing once burning CDs started. When they started burning my CDs, I got tired of going around beating people up. We used to go around to all the stores, everywhere we saw my pirated CD, and just flip the tables over and beat their asses. Yeah, I got tired of that, so I had to do what everybody else was doing, but I had to do it better.

I couldn't stop people from burning my CDs. I had made a few trips to other cities and they were doing the same thing. So I started burning twenty thousand CDs, and every show I went to, I would sell them hand to hand at ten dollars apiece. I used to make a cool sixty to seventy thousand dollars, and that was just off the mixtapes. I would sell them to the stores in Baton Rouge—you know, the regular stores—and all the record stores everywhere. I would make over sixty thousand dollars. That's how I first started hustling the burned CDs back in 2000–2003.

I had people in trucks going all across the southern regions and up north, just making drops to the stores for me. Those were the drops where they were bringing back fifteen to twenty thousand dollars like it was cocaine money, but it was legal business.

Those were some sweet times for me because I was young, twenty years old. I felt like I had beat the game and my music was steady spreading more and more. I remember an older woman told me, "I heard you talking about your music leaking. We buy your music out of the stores when we can, Boosie, we love you. But your music isn't in all the stores, so how can you feel like that? So us burning your music when we get it, it's like a blessing to you." Ever since that day, that just stuck with me.

I really thought deep about it. Yeah, I had been tripping. Why would I tell them to stop burning my CDs? Fifty percent of my fans weren't even buying my CDs out of the stores; they had them burned. So, after that, I was like, fuck it—because in 2003–2004, it was Boosie's burned CDs everywhere. When I say everywhere, you could go up to Wisconsin, all the way down to Georgia, and all you'd see was Boosie 1, 2, 3. They were Boosie all the way. It's Boosie 23 now. The good thing is they weren't the CDs from the stores.

Even though I was originally pissed about the burning CDs thing, I can say now, with a different mindset, I feel like the burning stage helped my career. I generated money on the back end because it got me famous everywhere. It got people all over onto my music. I was a hood legend. Those in the ghetto who can't buy music, they're gonna burn that shit. Now I see how burning widened my horizons.

Hip-hop makes it possible for a young Black artist to come up, because our culture wants to hear that voice. Everybody wants to know what the hood is like, especially people who have never been to it. Then there's also the people who have been through it and feel you deeply.

So, with that, I'm encouraging my Black people to come on now, try this music. You know it only takes one record to change your life. I always tell dudes that. You can't go to jail for rapping. Music is much different from selling dope. You can go on a computer, burn three hundred CDs, and sell them, and you won't go to jail. Don't get me wrong, I don't knock the hustlers, because I was one. I know how they have to get it. So I try to tell them we have to get it like *this*, and at the same time respect the grind.

The music has always been a part of Black people's lives. We had artists such as Nat King Cole, Sam Cooke, Jackie Wilson, and Nancy Wilson, moving through the era of Aretha Franklin, Harold Melvin, Marvin Gaye, and Bootsy Collins, to the likes of Michael Jackson and Prince. Music has a way of touching people's souls. It's what got our families through.

Some people just don't know what hip-hop did for Black people. They don't know that all of us were made from hip-hop—our mommas and daddies fucked off hip-hop. Hip-hop has gotten us through so much shit. You know what I'm saying? When we got beaten down by the police, when we got shot, who spoke up for us? Hip-hop. When we got muthafuckin' sprayed down, no politician spoke up for us. Rappers get the point across, point-blank.

Culture is what's happening right now. It's what you are seeing every day. You turn on the TV and see cops getting away with murder, you see fourteen-year-olds having babies—and when you express it, you're talking about our culture. You are talking about what is going on, and once you do that, you get power. N.W.A had it. Public Enemy had it.

People often ask me what we have to do to change our culture so it isn't generation after generation going through the same thing—and I'm not sure, we're so deep off in it. Where I was raised, the mommy teaches her daughter how to hold fools down. Then the daughter teaches her daughter how to hold fools down. I was thinking one day, *How do we break this cycle when everybody is doing the same thing?* Take Section 8—people, that shit is to break Black families up. That shit was designed to tear Blacks apart. If you are on Section 8 and they find out the daddy is living in the house, it's fraud. How do we make people see that the Section 8 rules are designed to keep the father out of the house? The world automatically thinks a Black person is trying to defraud the system, instead of trying to understand that the ends will never meet without a second income to supplement the needs of that family.

How can you say "We want world peace" when you won't legalize marijuana, but you've legalized alcohol? Alcohol kills more people in the world than anything, even more than guns. It kills more kids than anything else. Go to the stadium and divide it into half the people smoking marijuana and half alcoholics. How many fights do you think will break out on each side? Since I was a kid, I've been looking at liquor stores on every corner in my neighborhood. But when I go play UA with my white friends, I don't see liquor stores.

■ ■ ■

People refer to me as the mayor of Milwaukee. It's cities like Milwaukee and Jackson, Mississippi—they've never had a big rap star that came from their cities. I have been performing in their cities since I was fifteen years old, so when I come they say, "You're from here." It's a special kind of love. No one else was hollering Milwaukee. No one else was hollering at Jackson, Mobile, or Savannah. No one was hollering Baltimore or Duvall. When they had no one else repping their cities, they had me.

For decades, when you talked about anything from Louisiana, all you talked about was New Orleans. You didn't talk about Baton Rouge until Boosie Badazz. I made those muthafuckas. Now when you say Baton Rouge, it's got a stamp on it and that's real shit.

As a matter of fact, I was just reaching out to YoungBoy. I'm trying to start our own sports agency, so I've been waiting to see what we're going to put together. We're tired of hearing about everybody from Down South getting taken by all these sports agencies. We'll just start our own shit and get our own money, and everybody can come to us.

It would be an honor to teach my hustle to others. I would hate to see them young niggaz ain't got shit after rapping. They have put so much work into the industry and you know they thought they would make that money forever, but you can't rely on rap to make your money forever. Period. You going to be rapping at eighty-nine years old? Like, what the fuck?

If you don't spread your hustle from rap—and this applies to anything you do—you're going to be fuckin' broke in ten years. If that football player doesn't get that deodorant endorsement, or that other muthafuckin' deal, and that EA Sports contract, they're going to go broke, probably sooner than later.

If you're renting a house in L.A. at fifteen to twenty thousand dollars a month and you stop making hits, you have spent damn near four or five million dollars with these people, and now you're going to fail out. They're going to put you out after you paid them all that money. You should have just bought you some land and built your own home. You don't even know these people you're renting from— the property is handled by a management firm. If you ask them, "I just gave you four million dollars, can I be late one time on the rent?" they'll say, "Hell, no! I don't even know you, you're just a renter."

Do you feel what I'm saying? We have to look at ourselves and the choices we made when all this shit is gone. If you came out of your pocket and paid twenty thousand dollars a month for forty-eight months straight, you could have built a home for a million dollars and the shit would look like it cost you ten million. We have to look at that shit. You have to look at life from every angle and learn from your mistakes, so the negative gets turned into a positive.

That's what I am telling all my youngsters in the game. I always try to school them: "Try to get you some land and get yourself a home. When you lease a car, as soon as you leave the lot, the car loses value and they make another one every six months." I am trying to school these young cats on some real shit by using examples of the things they envy the most.

I needed to leave Louisiana because of the system. It wasn't based on other people there. I'm the fuckin' man in Louisiana and I have love for my city. That's straight up, but it's the consequences of the system that have tainted my name. Certain people will always have it in for me. I feel I've made it and I definitely don't want to have to fight the system anymore, so I went where everyone rode Bentleys like they were Hondas. Everyone had a gorgeous home and was living like a hardworking celeb should live. I don't want to stand out wherever I go because that brings trouble—from bad people plus from the bad people with badges.

My homie Pete told me to leave Baton Rouge five years before I went to prison. Every year he'd say to me, "Boosie, why don't you just leave here?" I had to respond the way my heart felt. But if you feel a certain way, hopefully you'll learn from your mistakes and eventually grow out of being defiant. Especially when the people you're defying have the right to kill you and not get charged.

I was telling my little partner, "You know, niggah, you can't be wearing Gucci belts. You can't be going to splash like that, niggah. You can't be trying to splash off five thousand dollars, niggah; five percent of your bag was spent on Gucci."

The first mansion I purchased, I only put half on it. A year later, I was sent to jail and I had to let it go. I couldn't take the shit with me. I had to let it go, so I knew one thing: *The next time I find a place to own, I'm going to make sure I own the land first, then I'll build a home. It will be worth five times the price I paid for it.* Let's say you buy a five-bedroom for three million dollars. Do you know they built that home for six hundred thousand, then sold it to you for three million? So if you have the money, you can do all that yourself, plus design your home the way you want it.

Own your own land! People, you can go buy forty or fifty acres for half a million dollars. Think about it, niggah, you've spent that on weed and foreign shit alone. It's all gone now and it isn't coming back. You don't even wear the same size clothes anymore. That foreign car lost value and now you're trying to sell it. Then you go do the same things all over again. You just have to get your priorities right; that's what this is about.

You've already spent your land money and you keep spending it on dumb shit. Niggah, if you have a ten-thousand-dollar weed habit, know that you're spending your land. Something has to give. Once you get some land, they can't take that away—you own the shit. I just went and bought the property next door, two hundred fifteen thousand dollars. It wasn't wasted on weed and Gucci, temporary shit.

Recently, I'd had a pretty good weekend. I made like ninety-six thousand dollars just from features. I had two back ends, two shows for forty thousand dollars, so I put sixty thousand dollars with all of that and purchased the land next door. Just like that, in four days, I had fifteen acres. I've already started digging my home on that property. If you're going to Vegas, you're definitely going to fuck off the bread, but fuck that shit. Get on the ground and keep your cash.

In over forty years of hip-hop, there are only a few of us who actually got on the business side of it. Some people think a little bigger than others. I based a lot of my hustle off being in prison and looking at Jay-Z and Puff Daddy. I came home thinking, *If Jay-Z can own his own cologne and Puff started his own clothing line, why can't I? Especially if everybody in the world is hollering, "Free Boosie"?*

I was basically saying, *I'm going to get my own liquor, clothes, and cologne. I'm going to do all this, because if they can do it, hell, so the fuck can I.* So, people, when you feel it in your heart that you are that person and that you have the capability of starting your own business, go for that shit. There are a lot of people feeling that way, but they never go for it.

I didn't have the means to do the deals myself, but I just said fuck it and went for it anyway. Once I'm done thinking shit through, if I know I'm going to profit, I'm going for it. I'm always thinking in the best interest of my kids. Most of my businesses are just about taking a percentage, and that's because of my babies. This little fuckin' money right here? Shit, I might fuck that up. I don't even want that. I have enough coins to be straight, so you can't pay me like no fuckin' model. I don't want no three hundred fifty thousand—I'd rather have five percent.

I love to see CEOs who capitalize off deals. I'm not a hater, I'm a gorilla to this shit. It's the same as the game—if this niggah has a plug and this niggah's plug is flooding the game, I need to get under his plug. That's what it's about, and I just love to see other niggaz in the game make power moves.

When I saw someone do shit with the schools, that had me thinking. Now I'm leaning towards getting my own school in Baton Rouge. I can just picture the way I'm going to have my school. I want to bring activities back to the schools—Ping-Pong championships, double Dutch championships, things of that nature. In the movie *Life of a King*, Cuba Gooding taught the kids life skills through the game of chess. He took a bunch of miscreants who the system wanted to throw away and changed their lives. Teaching and educating come in many forms, and not everyone has the knack to make someone want to listen to them. I want the youths to wake up every morning and want to go to school. But to have that, you gotta put activities in these kids' lives to draw them in. That's what Boosie is working on. That's one of my bucket list things. I want my own school.

When I first came home, I hooked back up with one of my business partners, Steven "Stevo" Love, to put together my first liquor deal. I remember the shit like it was yesterday. This man is as creative as ever and full of moneymaking ideas. He called me up and said he was about to shoot by the house so we could converse on some things. When he got there, he pitched this deal to me about having my own liquor. Of course I was game for it. First, we needed to come up with a name. Within minutes it was finalized: Boosie Juice. We took that shit and ran with it.

A lot of people ask me why I named it that. Simple: I own fifty percent of my brand and that's why I put my name on it. I was the first artist to put their name on a liquor bottle. Now, that's boss shit simply because I own it for real. No ambassador shit, making the next company rich. Fuck that! I'm about ownership, long-term money.

Next, Stevo and I did a cologne deal with Dangerous Cologne, where I received fifty percent of the profits. I also have the Rap Snacks chips. I have the Alkaline Lyfe water and the Jewel House clothing deals. One of the craziest deals was when Stevo and I hooked up with Kenny "Pimpin' Ken" Ivy to do a book deal with one of the biggest publishing companies in the world, Simon & Schuster. I was going to write the shit out of this book, so I teamed up Curtis "Mr. Galena" Butler and Charles "The StoryTellah" Burgess, two of the hottest authors to ever surface from the inner-city streets of Milwaukee. Not bad for a young Black man from the ghetto streets of Baton Rouge, Louisiana, aka Cross The Tracks.

■ ■ ■

When I came home, I was really focused. I wanted to take it up another level on the business side. It was all about getting more into the music. I knew how to do the music, but I was just trying to get other deals. I'd been trying to get a clothing line deal since forever. I was shopping one time back in '07, and Nick Cannon was trying to get someone to endorse me in a clothing deal. *Shout-out to Nick Cannon.* I don't think the people believed in me back then, but when I came home I was on boss stuff. I was ready. Since I had clout, I was going to talk to people. When I came home, niggaz was saying, "Boosie, you stayed solid, dog. You are definitely one of the real ones."

My music kept coming. People already knew where I was trying to go with this shit. I was just so focused on trying to get a bag, being as my shit had gotten fucked up while I was in prison. Most of my money had been spent on lawyers, and them muthafuckas had cost me a grip, so I was damn near drained. The rest of it was spent doing time and taking care of my family.

I have to say, though, my momma—man, that woman is truly my pride and joy. She had a little money put up and decided to hold on to it until they released the king back into the jungle. It was surprising because I didn't know Momma had shit when I came home, but I was wrong. Yeah, Momma had a little something for a niggah.

It is like that sometimes, you know, when you're paying off lawyers and all that shit. Believe me, it's for real when you are fighting a death row charge. I didn't really have anyone to help me. I had people who had to come up off their land, like Miss Savannah and Mr. Boykin of the NAACP. I had a lot of members of the NAACP with me. The white people were fighting to claim my life, so I needed some heavy hitters on my team and I recruited the best. I didn't really have anyone on speed dial who was willing to aid me financially, so I turned to those who had and will continue to have a voice that carries in this world.

When I did go to niggaz to ask for some coins, all I received were a bunch of confused expressions. They were shocked at me asking them for cash. It was good I had some money before I got sentenced;

that's how I was able to get some good lawyers. Plus, a niggah had a little change to hold me down until I could get back home.

That's how your boy hustles. I don't operate off pride. If I'm trying to get a beat made or a movie budget for something, I call the niggah I know who's sitting about a hundred million dollars strong or more. I'm like, "Hey, I got this on the table and I'm trying to woo da woo da woo . . ." That's how a niggah rolls; I'm a businessman. All it takes is one good heart to believe.

I saw one muthafuckin' billionaire on TV, a Chinese man, and I Googled his ass. I tried to get a meeting with him. That's how I always played the shit. I never thought I could fuck with the same old people and elevate. That's why I signed with who I signed with. Where I'm from you have to grab on to somebody or you're going to be selling dimes your whole fuckin' life. Just keep that in mind: you gotta grab on to somebody with more knowledge than you. Not only grab on but listen, because they didn't make it to where they are by not listening to someone else.

So, you know, I'm trying to fuck with billionaires. I ain't going to make no millions fuckin' with niggaz only making hundreds of thousands. I ain't going to make a billion fucking with no millionaire. I have to find me a billionaire and give him this perfect layout I have in my mind.

When I got out, my bro and I set up the Drew House, my clothing line deal. It was with some big-timers, some niggaz with a nice piece of money. I received twenty-five percent of the shit even though I had my own bag. I didn't get paid to put on clothes; naw, I had owner-ship. I get that ownership check in my name.

After that, Stevo and I did the Boosie Juice and we are mov-ing, dog. They might try to take me off the shelves in a minute. Like once you get off in the liquor business, Absolut, Hennessy, and shit like that are going to try to get rid of you. They didn't like it when I hit them with the Boosie Juice. The way I was doing it was like this: if you bought one hundred cases, I would come and do an in-store. That's how I got to jacking them muthafuckas off—one hundred cases, another hundred cases, another hundred cases, just like that.

After that I did the Boosie Chips with the Rap Snacks. It's fifty-fifty. I have two bags on the market right now. I got my chips and my cheese puffs. We can't forget about the cologne, Dangerous by Boosie Badazz. I get fifty-fifty off that also. I also have a percentage of a gold mine in Africa. I also got some shit in crypto right now.

I have my estate on forty acres. It has thirteen bedrooms, a full basketball court, an Olympic-size pool, a zip line, a football field, a volleyball/beachball court, and a two-story treehouse. I just bought the land next door, so that's fifteen more acres. I just bought that land and started building me a Batman mansion on it. I'm going to build it with the lights in the sky like in the Batman movies. I saw that when I was little, and I still want to live that dream.

All this was done in four years. I don't know how I did it, I just get motivated from my hustles. Like when I wake up, I go outside to have a smoke and look at the backyard. I start thinking about Cross the Tracks and shit, and I get really motivated by my hustle and all the things I could do for my children. Because the kids and I are going to ball all the fuckin' way out. That's what I wanted to do when I was little. I always wanted to go to the mall and say, "I can buy this." I just get so motivated, loving all that I have from the hustle.

The day I got out of jail, I started my own record label—it's called Badazz Music Syndicate. I can drive side projects and get all the money. I can get it and still be with Trill and the Atlantic game and still do me. That was big for me. I signed Yung Bleu and he's already got two gold albums. We're almost platinum. I signed him with Columbia. I've signed a lot of good talent, like Lil Blurry, B Will, and my son, Tootie Raww. Oh yeah, I've got my own phone too. I've got a deal on that, with Kurtis Blow. Can you believe that the legendary Kurtis Blow and I did a deal? He has a good head on his shoulders. He came to me with it and I was with it, so he and I have our own trap phone right now. Like I said, I'm just trying to keep knocking these deals down because that is the only thing that is going to have me eating forever.

My business education, such as dealing with CEOs, came from the streets. Me having bad paperwork was what smartened me up. Reading books took me to higher levels as well. Just being in the industry, you'll find yourself around people you know who will make mistakes and you'll see them fail; that will make you smarter. You should know you can't do what they did. If you see six or seven people fail, it should be hard for you to fail like that—to be the eighth person to fail the same way. That came from me having longevity in the game. I started doing this in '98, so there ain't too many left but me, Lil Wayne, and Jay-Z.

I've also started doing movies. I was just in theaters in the *Glass Jaw* movie. I played the character Rico, a boxing promoter who ran an underground boxing ring. Live-ass movie; you need to go check it out. You know I did the *Ghetto Stories* movie also. So, yeah, I'm going to be deep into films. I got Badazz Films going right now. I also start shooting my biopic, *My Struggle*, a story of Boosie Badazz, in a couple of weeks.

I'm trying to shoot at least three movies in 2020 and just keep on pushing. I'm doing it myself. At first, I went trying to get the money for the films, but nobody believed in me, so I'm doing them myself. I'm putting together some great work, and I'm trying to get this film money the right way.

Before I was trying to do *My Struggle*, I tried reaching out to niggaz: "Give me fifteen hundred dollars and I'll give you fifteen or twenty thousand back," and niggaz wouldn't even do that shit. And at that moment, I told my partner, "Man, I'm going to get a tattoo that says 'The Boss of All Bosses' on my back." I told him that shit like two months ago. I didn't want to spend the money on the movie by myself. You see what it is? Everything happens for a reason. If it wasn't supposed to go like that, it wouldn't have happened like that. I read my horoscope one day, and it said something like, "Don't pressure yourself about this situation. Your story will be sold and you will profit from your authenticity." So I felt like I was saying, *Fuck all that shit. You're doing that shit yourself. People will buy your story just for the story.*

I started my script in prison. I finished it six months after I got out, but I wrote the majority of it in prison. It took me nine months to write it, and I put my extra little twist on it about the cancer. I had to write it all out by hand. There were no typewriters in there.

I want the younger generation to just keep going. Keep going! If you are involved in music, make a hit record. That's what it's about. To the younger generation who's chasing my dream, I tell them, "Make hits, because you don't know how long you have in these streets to live as a rapper." Rappers, we have the most dangerous job in America. I feel that way, especially in my hometown. I tell them to make those hit records and skip everything else.

If you make all these records and they are just regular records, it takes too long. You'll get fucked trying to record thirty-five songs. You have to work on that one muthafuckin' song and lace that bitch, then move on to the next one. By the time you're done, you're gonna have like eight songs done. I tell that to artists because I don't want them to be local rappers for eight years. I don't like that shit, because they get frustrated with themselves and get to asking you what they didn't do. What you didn't *do* is make a hit record! Once you make that hit record, somebody is going to hear it and come and get it.

A hit is a hit, that's something that can't be denied. So, all you youngsters out there, make hits. Don't go in those studios on bullshit; go in there and make a hit. You have to make those hits and you'll pass everybody else. Then, you can't allow that hit to be your downfall. You have to go for the next hit.

I've been wanting to do a book about my life, so this is a blessing. In life, we learn about two things that are important: time and opportunity. When this opportunity came, it came at the perfect time. I wanted to make a statement with the book, so I teamed up with Stevo and he told me he had the perfect writers to help put my story on paper. He introduced me to two gifted brothers from Milwaukee. Mr. Galena is the author of *The Duffle Bag Boyz*, which is one of the hottest hood trilogies ever written. Then there's The StoryTellah, author of *Sins of the 7eventh*. After sitting down with them, I knew I was about to shock the world.

What I want people to get out of this book is that your time is coming. Not when you think it's time, but when God knows it's time. You see that after all this time and all my trials and tribulations with the law, cancer, diabetes, raising a family, and touring, you see Boosie's time came. You should have renewed faith that your time is coming and you should pray. What God has for you, no man can stop it.

My brother came to me informing about this new artist MO3 that had skills and was opening up for one of my shows. He said the cat was so good that he was thinking about signing him. One day we were in the shoe store and I was finally introduced to him. We shook hands, and I told him that my brother was thinking about signing him and I was all for it. I said that somebody needs to be making money when I'm not, so it might as well be him. I have to admit that the boy was a natural superstar. The way he moved the crowd through his music was something to see. He had this way about him that people just loved. At the same time, there was a portion of people that hated his ways.

As time progressed, people began showing their true colors. MO3 began having a lot of internet beef. Dudes were coming at him all the time. I'm guessing mainly because of his success—the boy took off like a rocket. I knew that the sky was the limit if he had the Boosie movement behind him.

I never got the chance to sign him, but I supported him all the way. He was doing his thing. His shows were selling out and his fan base had taken off. His managers were getting boatloads of requests from other rappers for features. As time passed, we became the best of friends. MO3 would often call me detailing his day. He was loving the good life, but the haters were beginning to make him feel a little uncomfortable.

With me having experience being under the spotlight, I knew exactly where he was coming from. I always told him to treat his haters like glass and look right through them. I explained that it's all part of success. You have to take the bad with the good. Little did I know that things had escalated.

During times of trials and tribulations, I tried to keep him close to me for his safety. We had a ball while spending time together. I was able to meet with a lot of his people and he with mine. We actually became closer than we expected.

One day he was driving northbound on I-35. He was riding solo and unarmed. It's said that the man who murdered him was traveling in the same direction. News reports said that the gunman exited his vehicle in an attempt to approach MO3's vehicle from behind. Witnesses say that MO3 spotted the assailant and responded by exiting his vehicle, fleeing, and seeking help. Before he was able to obtain any, he was shot in the back of the head in broad daylight. Onlookers were left speechless.

Once the news finally reached me, it was like a blow to the chest. Most folks might think that my concerns are more on business, but understand we were close. I didn't have any money invested in him. Naw, that was my niggah for real. I had gotten close to his loved ones and I couldn't imagine what his people were going through. I mean, we all come to a point in life where we lose an immediate family member, but the process is different for everyone. I let the family know that I was there for them in any way they may need me.

A few days had passed and MO3's family decided to put together a vigil in memory of him. I felt it was only right for me to be in attendance, being a good friend. When I heard shots being fired, I couldn't believe it. So many innocent people were present, and folks began scattering. My dumb ass was trying to be this upstanding citizen, so I started ushering people to safety. Before I knew it, I was shot and lying on the ground bleeding. I'm a little niggah, so the shit ripped right through me. I could only hope someone would come to my aid.

I ended up going to the hospital for the gunshot wound, and the fact that I am a diabetic added even more tension to the situation. At first they were talking about amputating my leg, but I was like, *Are you fucking serious?* That shit didn't set well with me. I couldn't see that vision at all.

Remember how I explained earlier that I am a prayer warrior? That incident opened up a conversation with the Man Upstairs like never before. Night and day I cried, begged, and pleaded for mercy and grace. One thing I've learned in life is that no matter what type of storm appears, God and God alone has the power that can change time.

Once the tests came back, the doctor informed me that there was a fifty-fifty chance of me coming out of this in one piece. Of course with God at the wheel I knew everything was going to be all right. He judges us by our hearts and he knew where mine was at.

The surgery was a blessing. I won't say it was successful, because that would be giving man the credit. All the praise, glory, and thanks had to be given to the Man Upstairs. Had he not placed His hands on me I wouldn't be here today. I also want to thank those whose prayers reached His throne.

I know my time is coming to do greater things. I want people to have hope after reading this book. I want them to get past the stage of visualizing dreams, stop procrastinating, and start manifesting their dreams into the realities they can have with a little faith and hard work. You can wait for a big star to come and help you, or you can do what it takes to be the next big star. Only you can bring that shit to life and become a boss. I want you to see what I've been through and say, "Oh, yeah, if Boosie can survive every pitfall, I'm definitely next."

One thing I don't want is for people to read this book and think I'm glorifying the drug game. *That is not the message.* If you're reading this book, this is the message: *You're next.*

The world is full of Lil Boosies. No matter how good and God-oriented you may think you are, no mortal man has walked this Earth perfectly. That's why the Bible tells us that God searched the Earth looking to find one made perfect and without any blemishes, but found none. So being the just God that He is, he sent his Son, who was made of flesh and bone, to be an instruction on how we are to live.

Many of the situations in our lives are brought on because of our actions. The way we think, act, and operate affects our present lives and our futures. A new generation has surfaced and the old one is fading away. As an experienced people, we must instill true values in our children so the new world being rebuilt will be better than the old one being destroyed.

"Train up a child in the way he should go,

and when he is old he will not depart from it."

—*PROVERBS 22:6*

ACKNOWLEDGMENTS

Special thanks to those who helped me put this project together. Thanks to my book agents, Steven Love and Ken Ivy, from Ivy & Love Literary Agency LLC, for making this book happen.